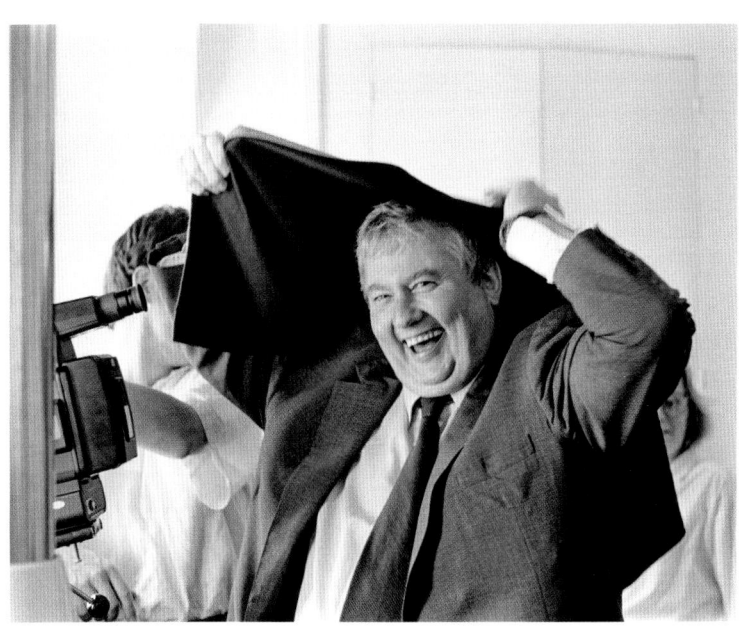

TERENCE DONOVAN
ONE HUNDRED FACES

EDITED BY
DIANA DONOVAN
DAVID HILLMAN

INTRODUCTION
PHILIPPE GARNER

ARCHIVE RESEARCH
ALEX ANTHONY

OH EDITIONS

Train hard, fight easy

Where do I begin, if I explain the unique force of nature that was Terence Donovan? What made him such a natural as a photographer, particularly of people? How did the gods conspire to endow this particular East End kid with the mix of curiosity, compassion, drive, generosity, humour, and sheer native savviness that made him so special and engaging a character and gave him the key to so productive and extraordinary a life? Perhaps a good place to start might be at the end, with a recollection of the immensely moving memorial service that celebrated his exceptional life.

On the 10th of March, 1997, St George's Church, Hanover Square, was packed to capacity with family, friends, and associates from all areas of Terry's life – notable among them Diana, Princess of Wales and Margaret Thatcher – and including prominent personalities from the worlds of fashion and the media, representatives of the Brigade of Gurkhas, and fellow judo enthusiasts. The music, reflecting Terry's Catholic ear, was as diverse as the guest list – from Sibelius, via Django Reinhardt and Stéphane Grappelli, to Willie Nelson's 'On the Road Again', played, I recall, as it should be, at maximum volume to overwhelm your senses. The one consistent element was the message that ran through the various tributes – a message of deep fondness and very considerable respect.

Lord Puttnam noted 'the extraordinary number and diversity of people crammed into this church', and evoked 'a steady, strong light that never seemed to flicker or waver'. He talked of loyalty, of generosity, and of 'glittering professional qualities' in 'the most amusing and inventive companion that anyone could ever wish for'. Lord Palumbo told of 'the warmth of that huge personality', and described Terry as someone with 'a profound understanding of the human condition and a deep well of tranquillity at the core of his being. Because of this he was quizzical, tolerant, and immensely wise.' Judo associate Syd Hoare read a doka, or 'poem of the way', by one of judo's great masters that Terry often quoted:

Freedom in continuous change
The heart should be like a bright mirror
Polished a thousand times
And rely on God-like speed and courage.

Terry Donovan Jnr read verses from a 3rd century BC

Buddhist text his father had recommended he read when he was eighteen. These closed with the suggestion:

*Better than a hundred years lived in idleness
and in weakness
is a single day of life lived with courage
and powerful striving.*

The testimonials and readings reminded us how Terry had built a profound personal philosophy for life, a wisdom that drew on his very wide experience. Above all, he believed in the huge possibilities that could flow from the alignment of fearless determination, open mind, positive attitude, and hard work. And he always found unexpected, memorable ways of conveying ideas in a few wise words, such as his advice, surely born of his judo practice, 'Don't forget: train hard, fight easy.'

Terry enjoyed driving around London, the city he loved. A photographer friend who had known him and appreciated his spirit and integrity told me recently of an incident from many years ago. Terry had suggested that he pick him up and they drive into the East End. The car was Terry's gleaming Rolls Royce – not exactly the vehicle in which to avoid attention in that run-down part of London. When the car slowed at a junction, a youth, resentful at the intrusive show of wealth, called out, 'Why don't you fuck off home!' Terry's spontaneous retort was 'I am home, c**t!' He could be forthright when necessary. The unexpected riposte, embellished with a blunt four-letter expletive, silenced the youth foolish enough to challenge this gentle but nonetheless formidable character. The encounter is a telling reminder of the arc of Terry's life – from working-class anonymity in Stepney in the East End to a grand West End send-off, in the heart of Mayfair, honouring a life of extraordinary opportunities seized and encounters enjoyed, to which the present volume bears such vibrant witness.

Terry's formal education was perfunctory, much of his boyhood spent on the road with his lorry-driver father. Aged eleven, and following in the footsteps of his uncle Joe, he apprenticed at the School of Photo-engraving in Fleet Street. Fascinated by watching images reveal themselves in the printing process, his next step was a logical one, as a photographer's assistant. After mandatory National Service, Terry soon found a job with fashion photographer John French, who ran an efficient and respected studio working principally for the daily press rather than the more prestigious fashion magazines. But his work was no less sophisticated. In fact, French, with his sure eye for pose and for lighting, set a new standard in this medium, making elegant pictures with tonal values that could overcome the limitations of newsprint. Terry had found himself a first-rate master. Serendipity, and the thirst for knowledge that fuelled his natural drive, had served him well. In 1959, he set up his own studio in Knightsbridge.

As an ambitious young commercial photographer specialising in fashion, portraiture and advertising, Terry was in the right place at the right time. He was to capitalise on the multiple strands of an emerging fashion, media, and cultural scene that made London's reputation in the sixties. Terry hit the ground running; his energy, sharp eye, and lively imagination, plus a charm that made it a pleasure to work with him, ensured his success. A new generation of magazines provided a fresh and adventurous showcase for a new breed of photographer. These publications were led by the revamped *Queen* and *Man About Town* (soon shortened to

About Town, then *Town*) and by the mass-circulation
colour supplements initiated by *The Sunday Times*
in February 1962 and soon followed by *The Observer*
and *The Telegraph*.

Much has been made of the trio of Bailey,
Donovan and Duffy, ever since the 10th of May, 1964,
Sunday Times Colour Magazine feature, 'The Model
Makers', in which Francis Wyndham wrote, 'The
London idea of style in the 1960s has been adjusted to
a certain way of looking, which is to some extent the
creation of three young men, all from the East End.'
Beyond their vaunted common threads of modest
origins, heterosexuality, and a youthful irreverence,
each found his own distinct way of working, while
rejecting the staged grandeur of traditional fashion
photography and the protocols of formal studio
portraiture. Terry soon proved himself a master of the
seemingly informal. He staged fashion shoots as if
they were reportage stories or scenes from gritty mov-
ies, notably ground-breaking male fashion stories. And
he made a speciality of studies of beautiful women –
models and actresses – whose appeal seemed natural
and effortless. His images, often grainy 35mm shots,
were of a disarming simplicity and seeming spontaneity
that belied the sensitivity required to make them. His
achievement in this area was commemorated in a
1964 publication to celebrate his 1963 Designers and
Art Directors Award. It is a one-of-a-kind gem that
includes portraits of Claudia Cardinale, Julie Christie,
Celia Hammond, Susan Hampshire, Jill Kennington, Sophia Loren and Sarah Miles. A text by the
photographer runs, unbroken by punctuation,
across the lower edge of cover and pages, giving the
volume a title, 'Women throooo the eyes of smudger
Terence Donovan....'

Terry was to build an impressive portfolio of

portraits through the years. To my eye, the simpler his pictures the better. All hinges on the magic ingredient that underpins their enduring interest. This has less to do with setting, styling or technical skill – that should be a given for any practitioner – and everything to do with human chemistry. If Terry's portraits hold our eye and convey a real sense of their subjects, it is because he has put them at their ease, subtly coaxed them to reveal themselves to his lens. And if charm and humour are surely key to this process, so too is the authenticity of Terry's engagement. We can sense that he is not just after a picture as a kind of trophy; we know he has connected and the resulting portrait is evidence of Terry's genuine curiosity and his empathy.

In a quite different context, explaining in 1990 the making of his bold, gestural black ink paintings that he called 'Chusin', meaning 'middle of the spirit' in Japanese, Terry gave an insight into his creative process: 'There was a moment when I started to be intrigued by the random yet controlled shapes of water on stone. I began to rearrange a pool of water on the stone floor of our kitchen, after an accident with fluid. The process of rearranging became fascinating and mysterious and oddly satisfying. It was a point of outstanding excitement when I first tried the process with dense black ink and paper.... It is an odd thing that when you neither drink alcohol nor take drugs, the power of colour and shape seem to have a metaphysical intensity that only pure un-chemical excitement can bring.'

In front of a blank sheet of paper, on the judo mat, or behind the lens, Terry brought to bear the combination of intense focus and dynamic action that defined his being and determined his ability to fulfil his objectives to such considerable effect.

Terence Stamp

18 August 1966

10

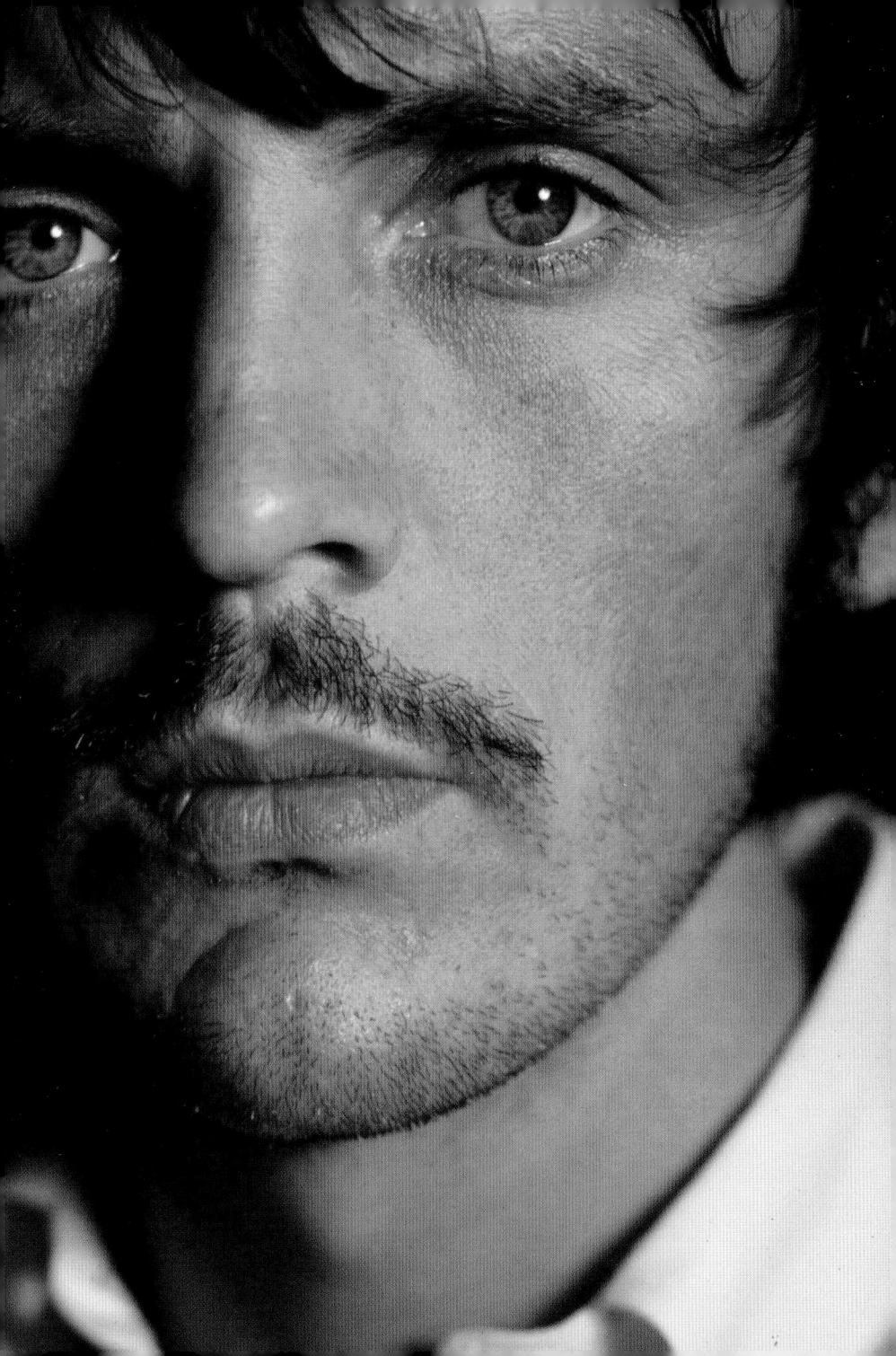

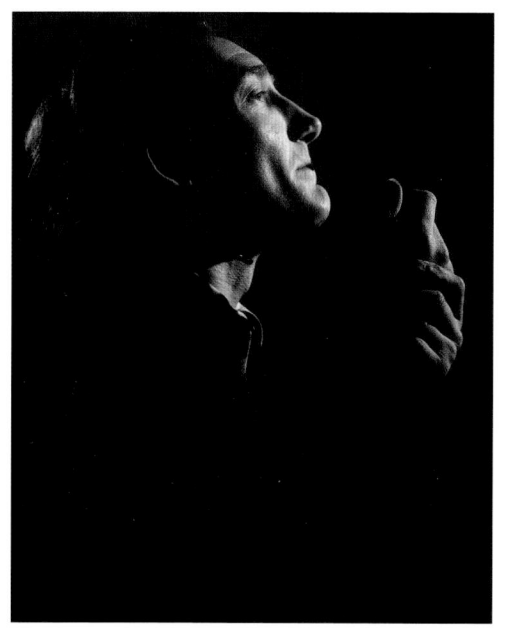

Albert Miller
1951
Terence Donovan's first portrait

Right
Osbert Lancaster
British *Vogue*
June 1978

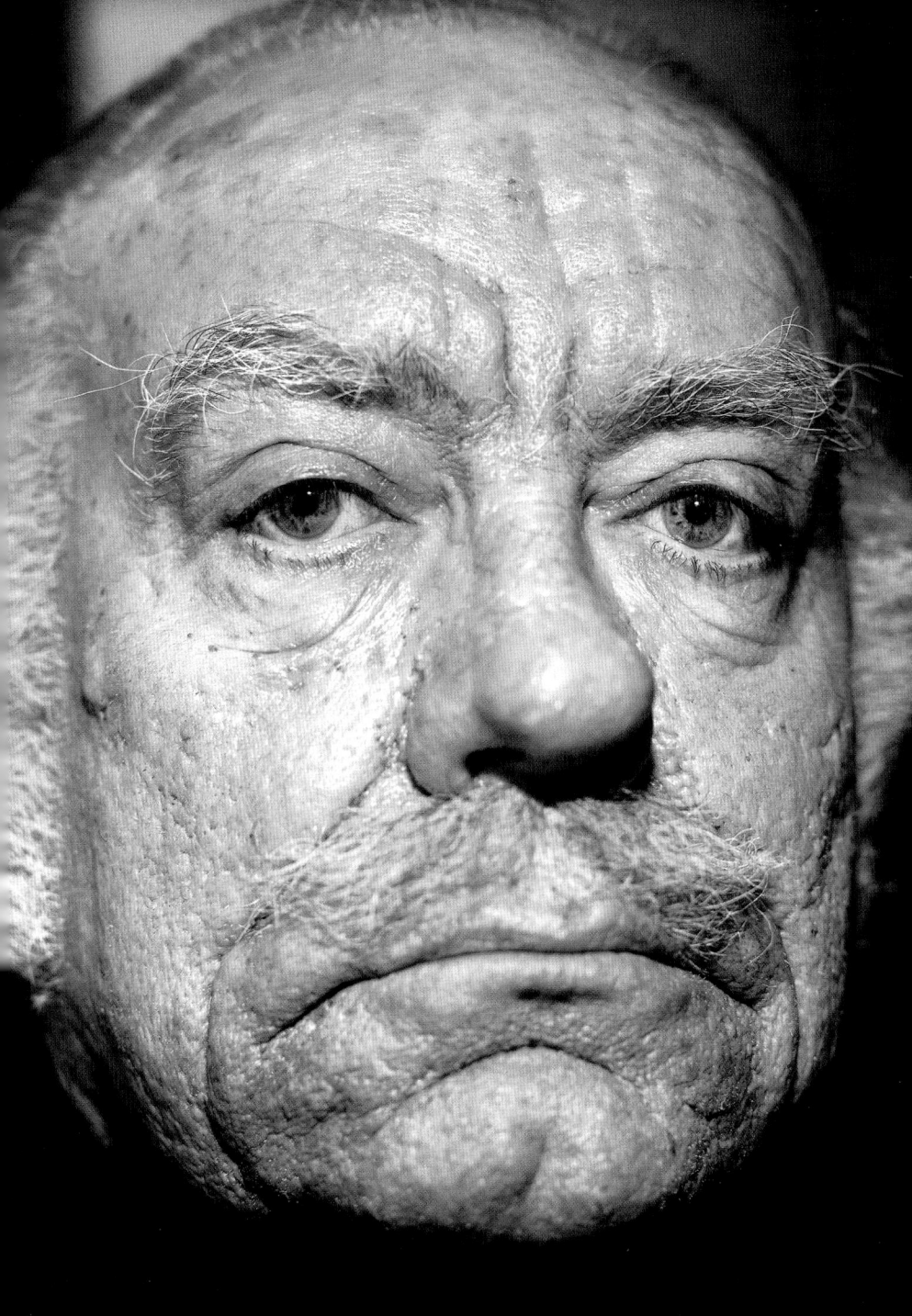

Overleaf
Celia Hammond
Queen
18 December 1961

Sophia Loren
Queen
May 1963
On the set of Anthony Mann's
The Fall of the Roman Empire

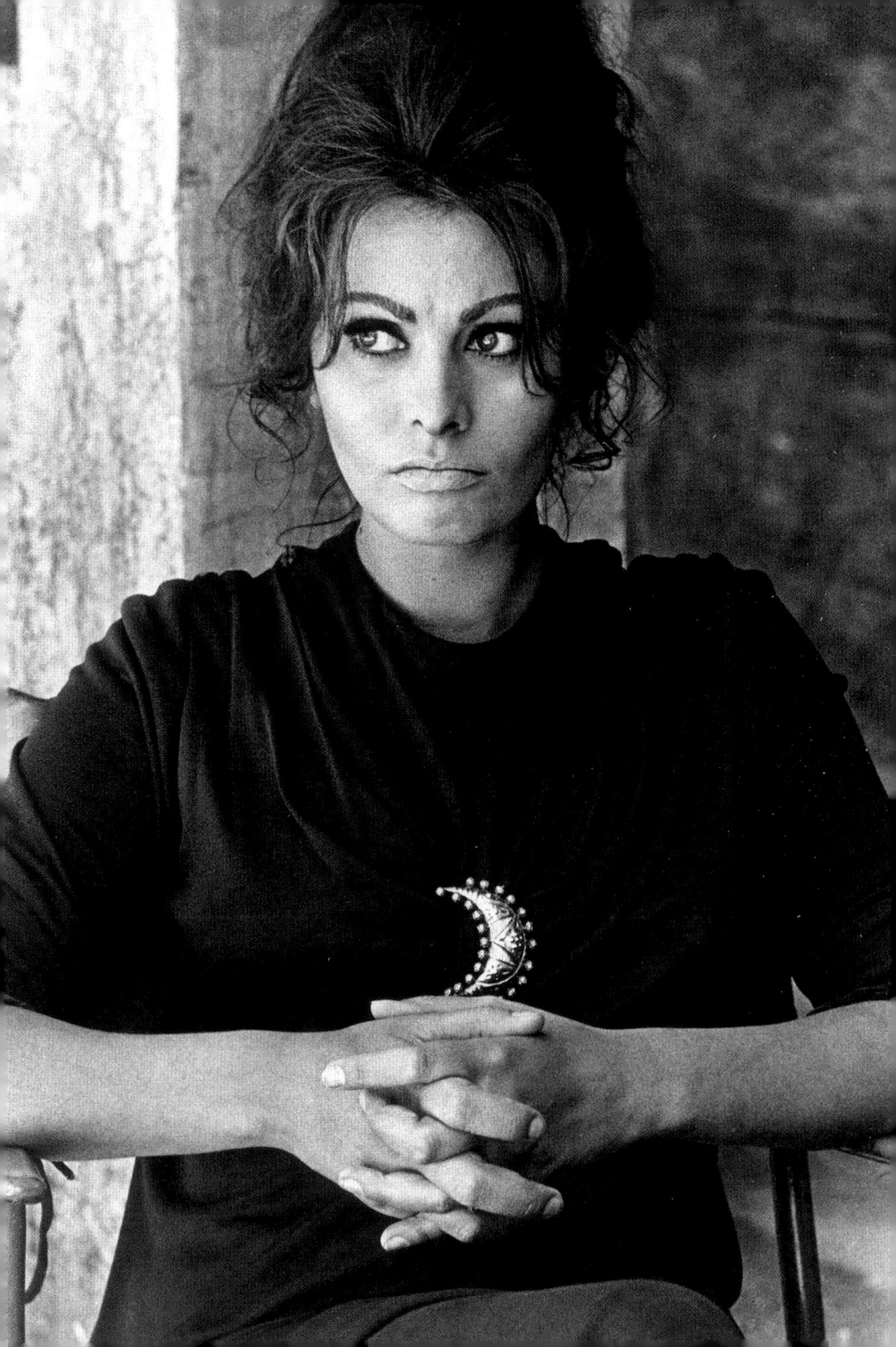

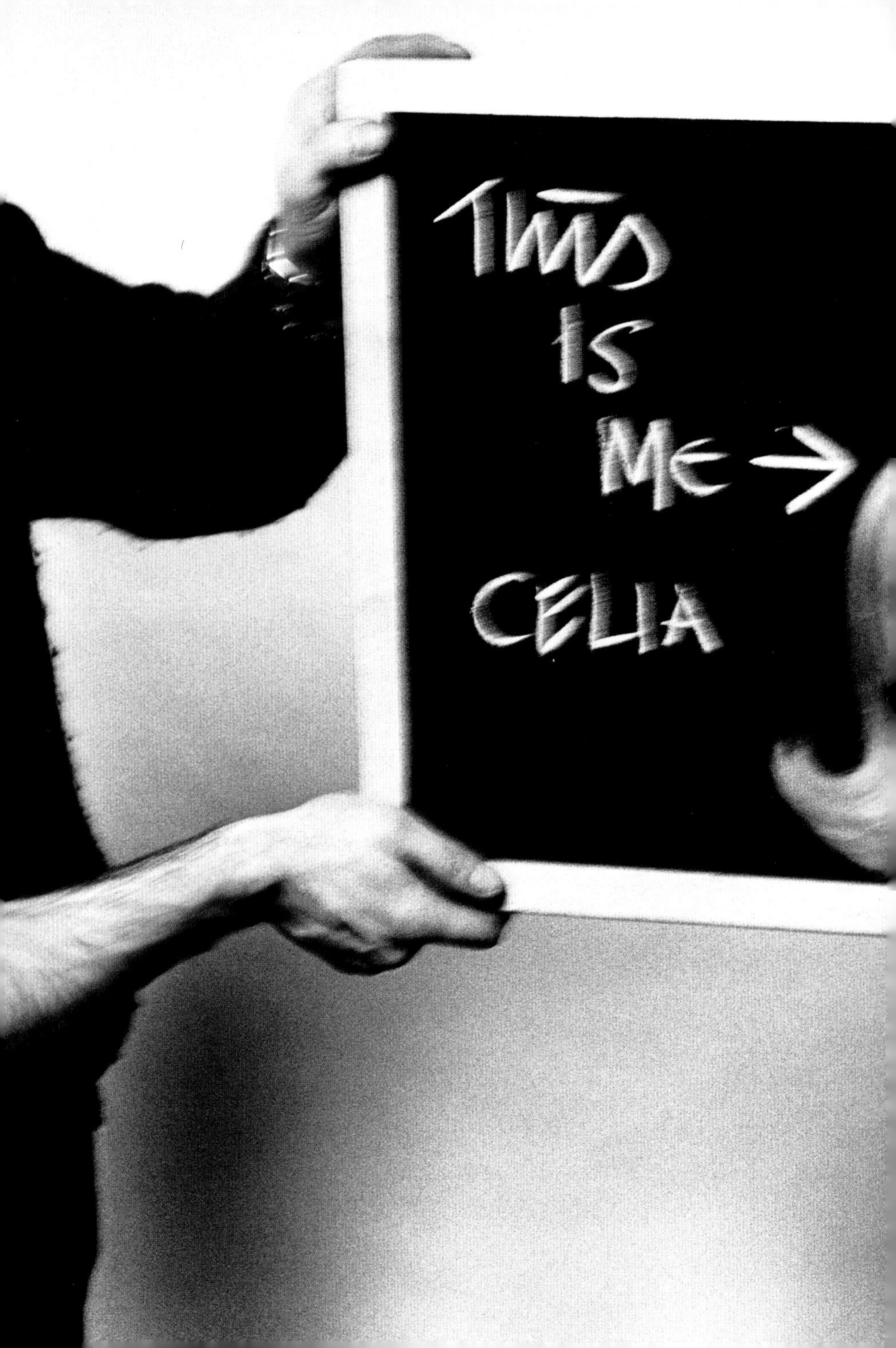
This
is
Me →
CELIA

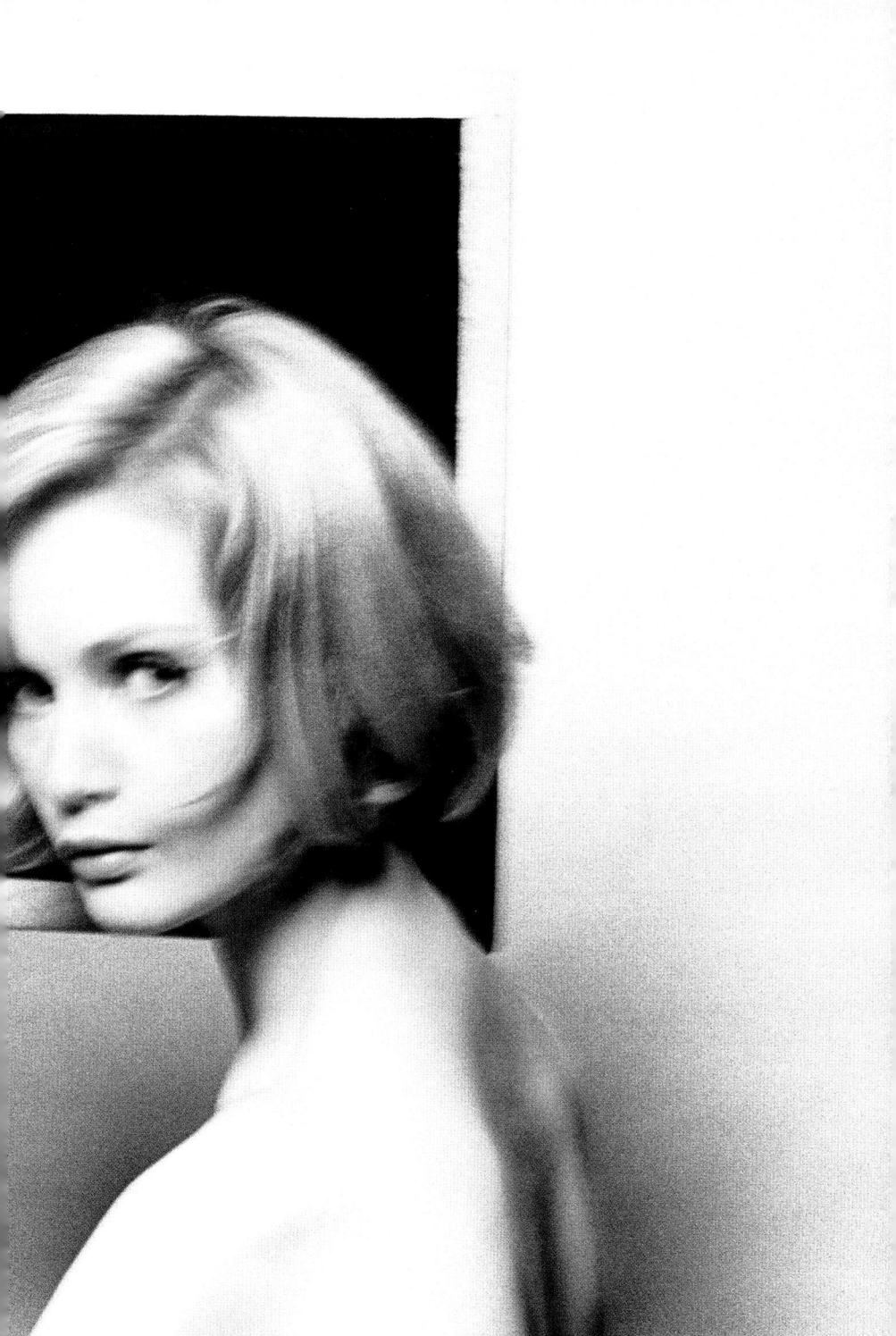

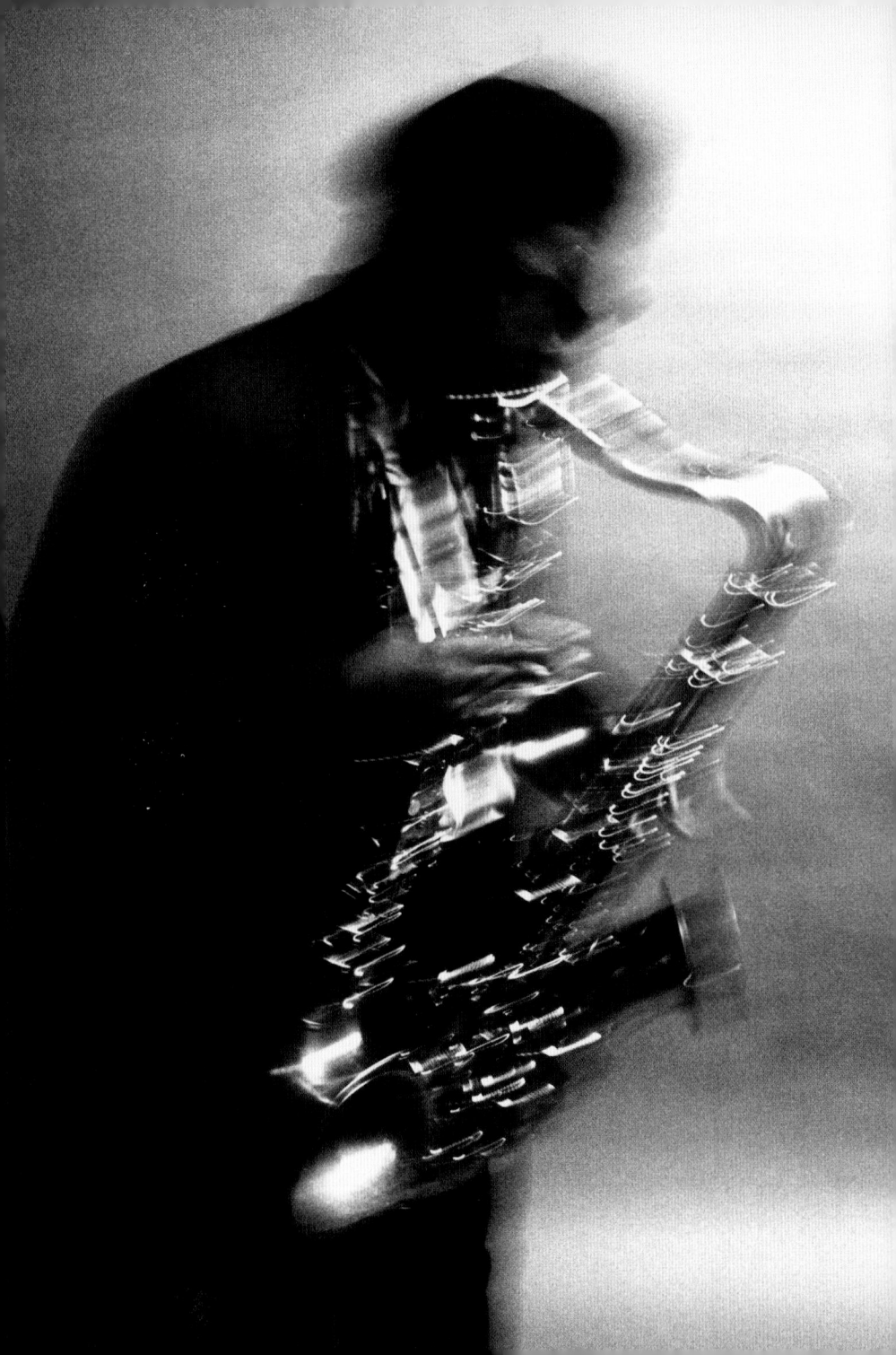

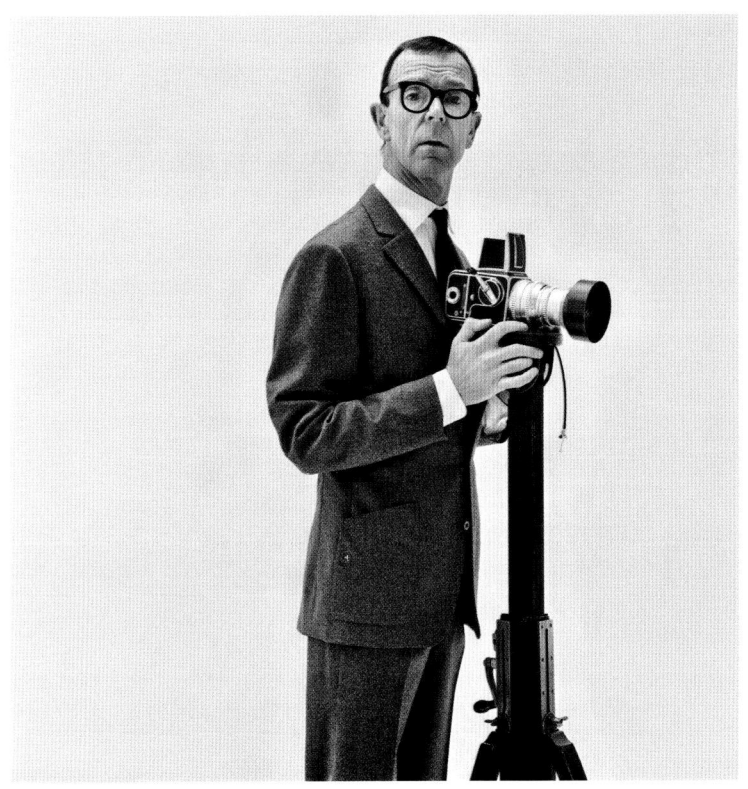

Roland Kirk
27 September 1963

Above
John French
Ilford advertisement
13 April 1965

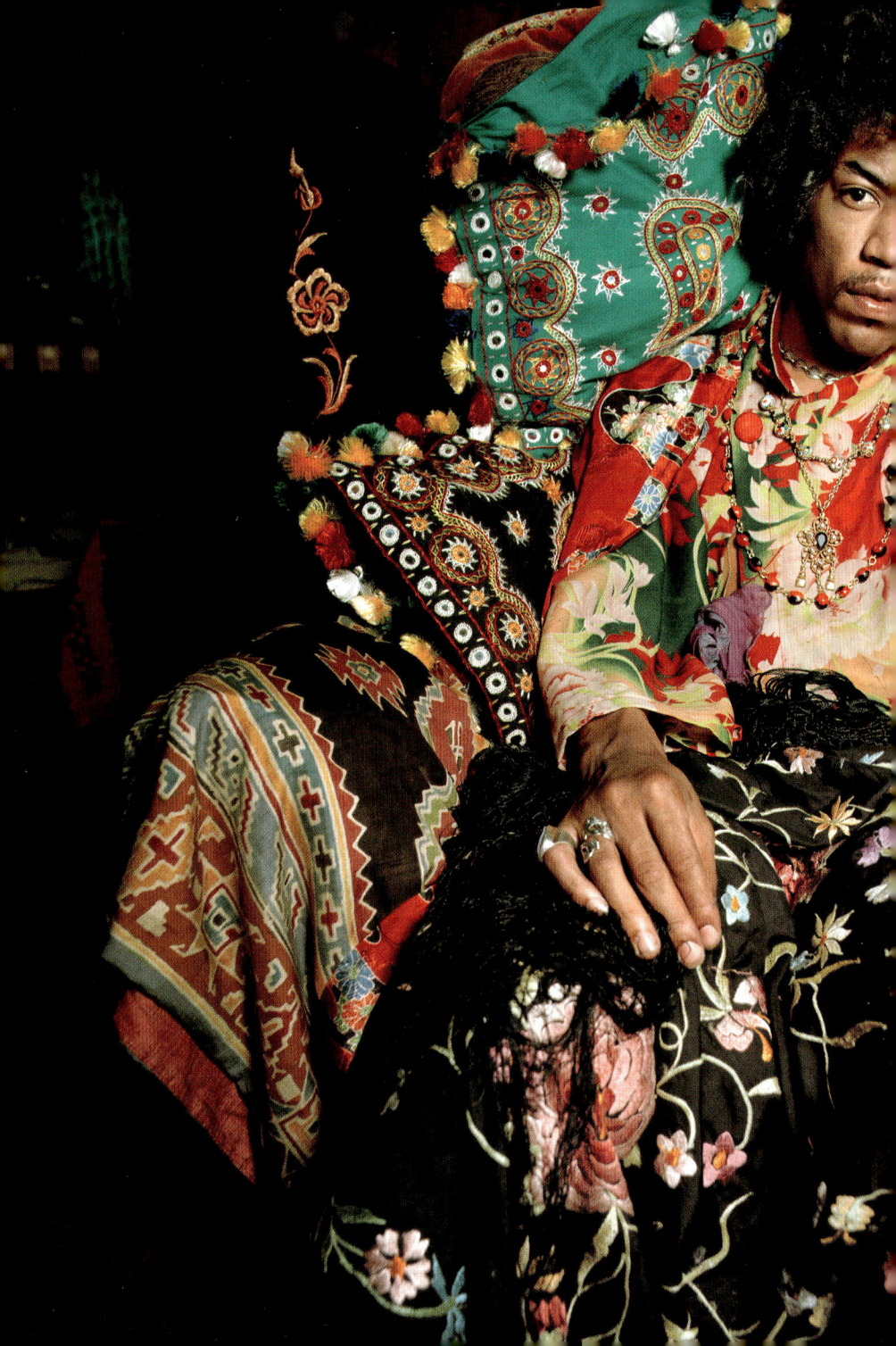

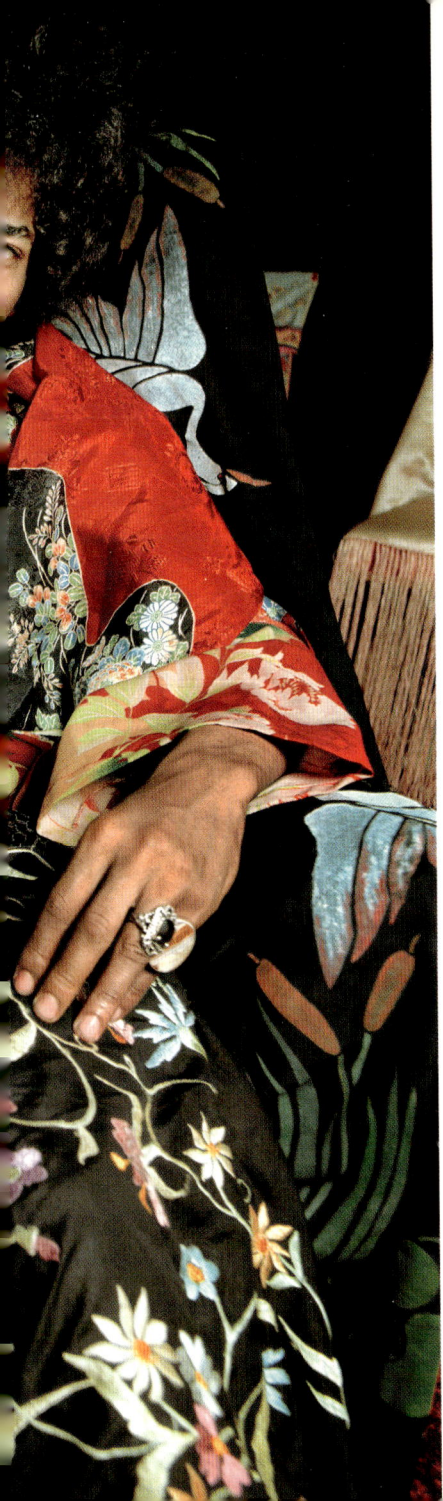

Jimi Hendrix
Observer Magazine
3 December 1967

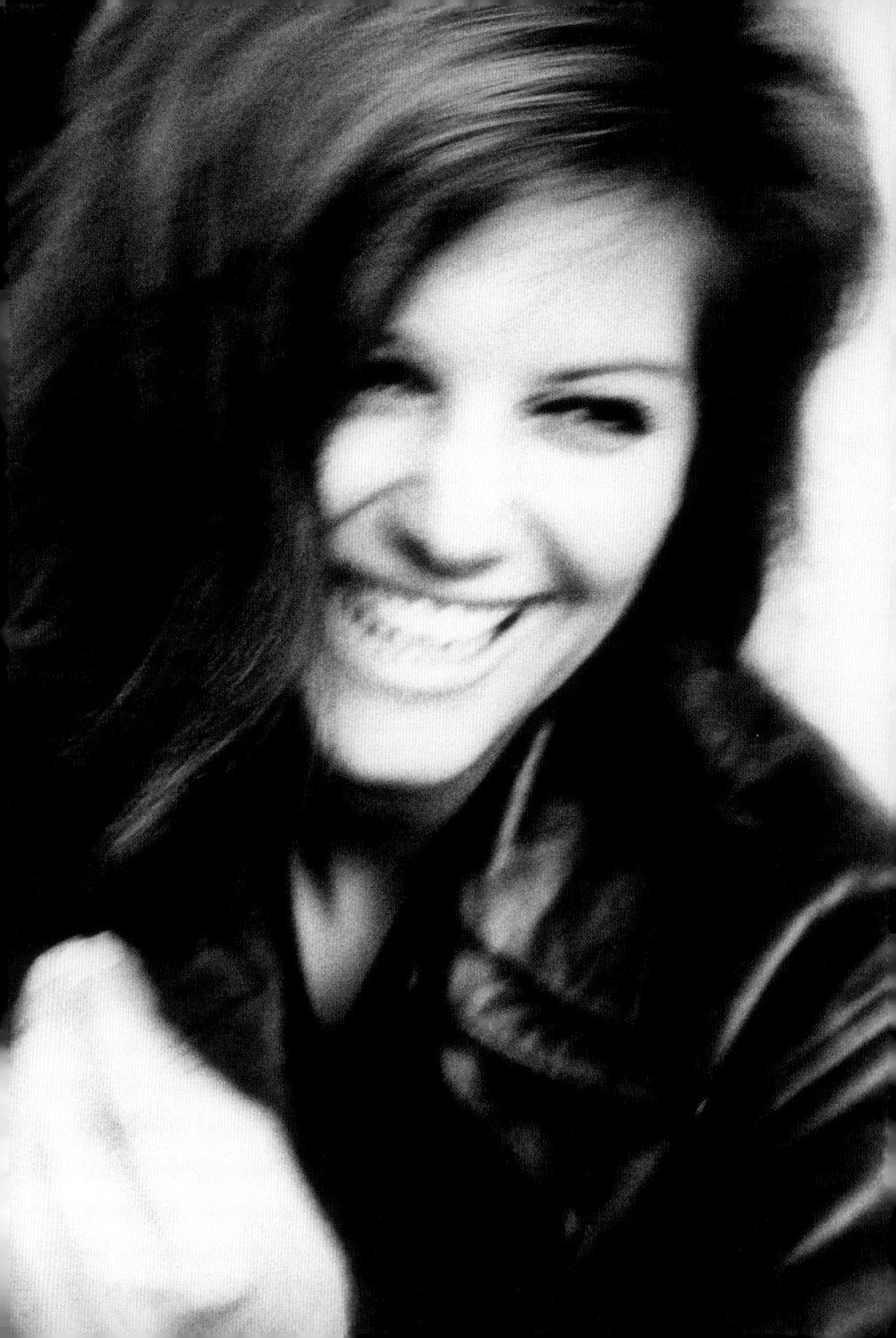

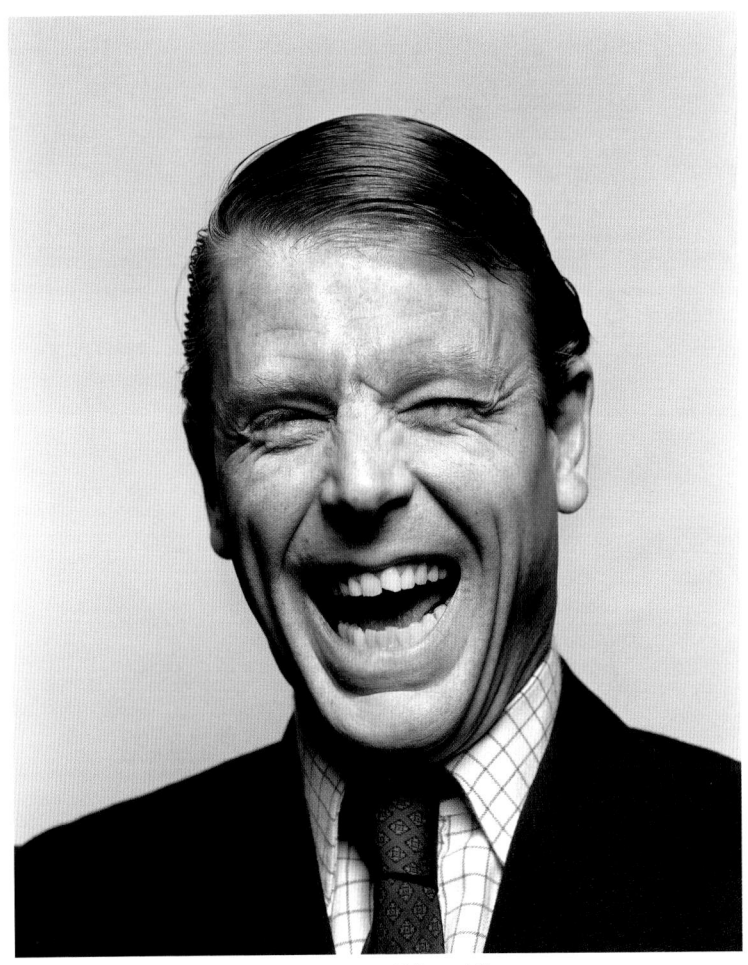

Claudia Cardinale
About Town
June 1962

Edward Fox
Cosmopolitan
26 January 1979

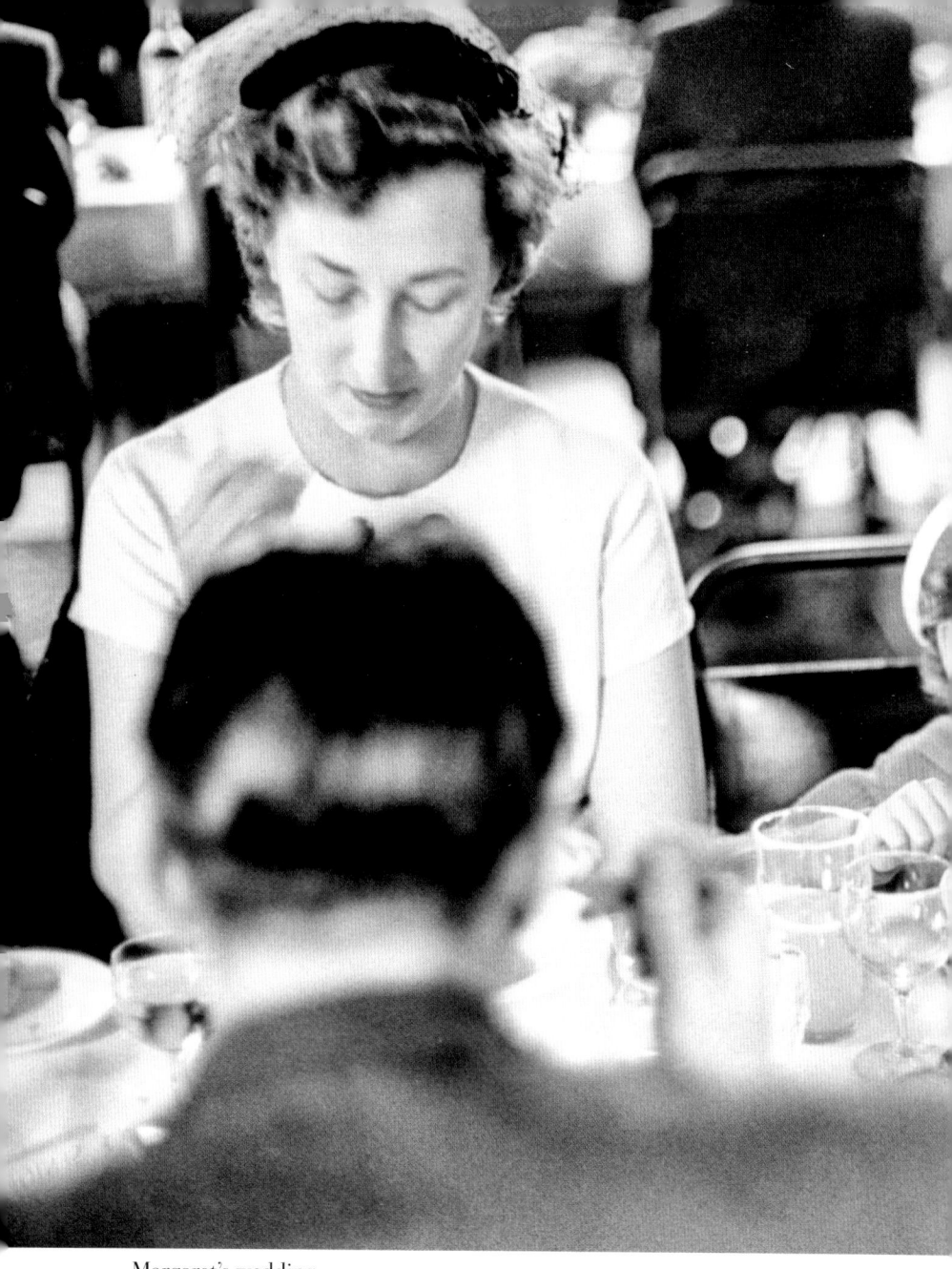

Margaret's wedding
17 September 1960

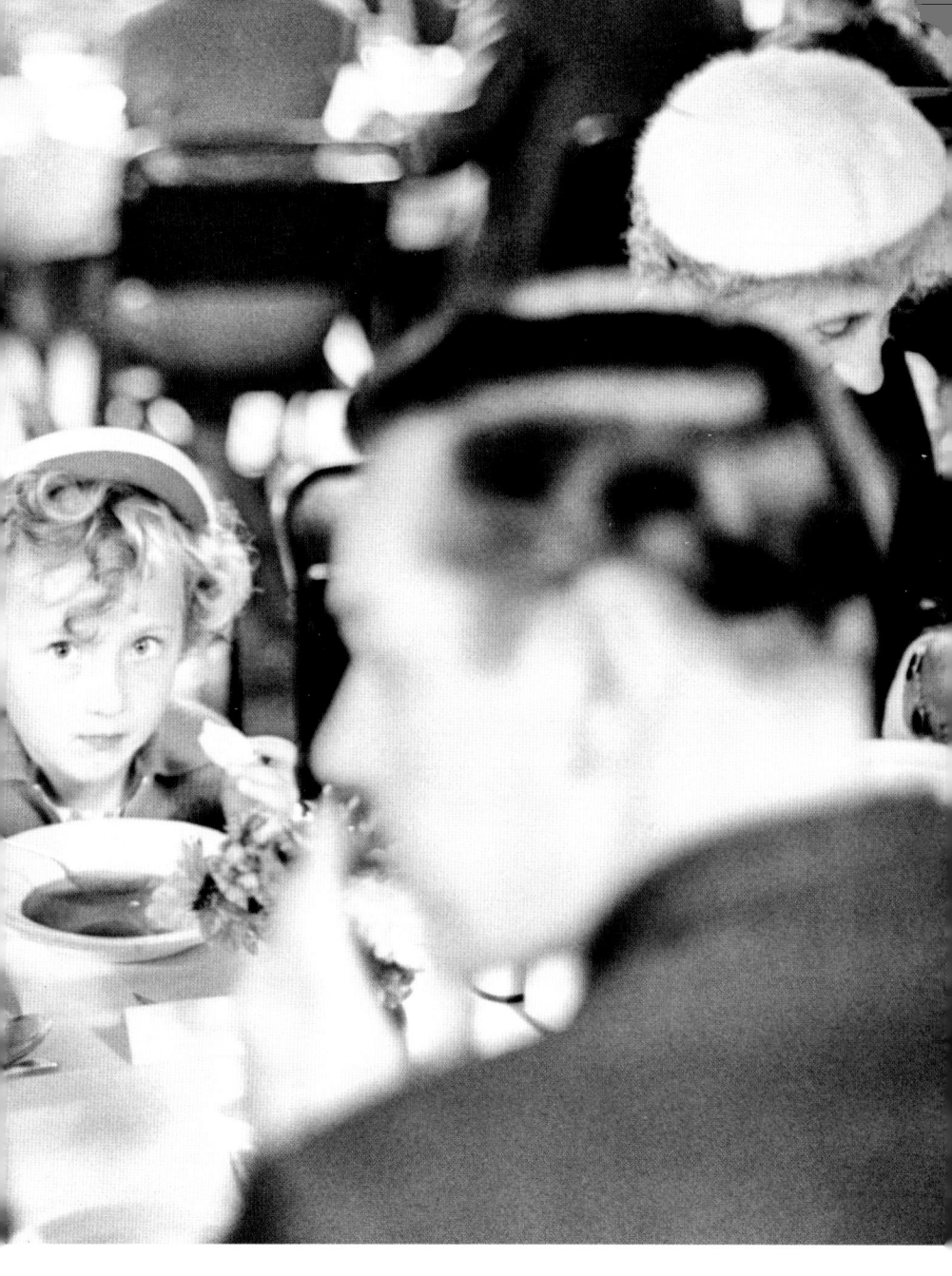

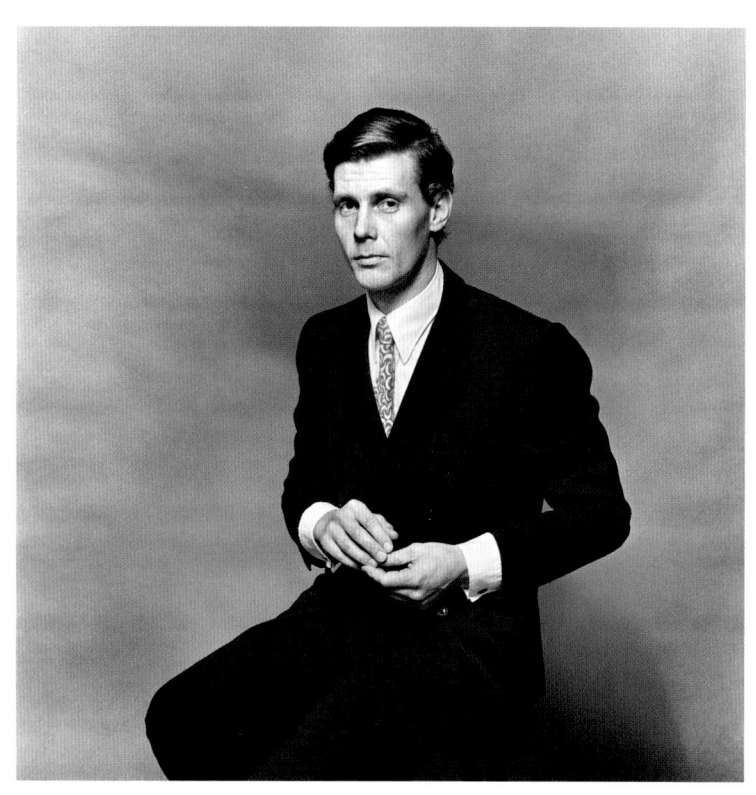

James Fox
8 December 1969

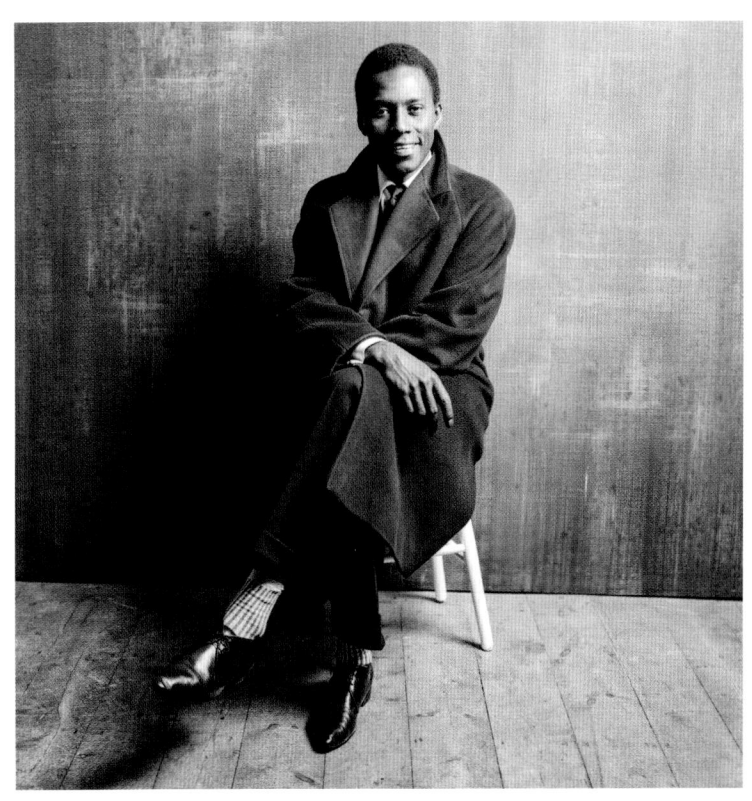

Johnny Secker
1 March 1961

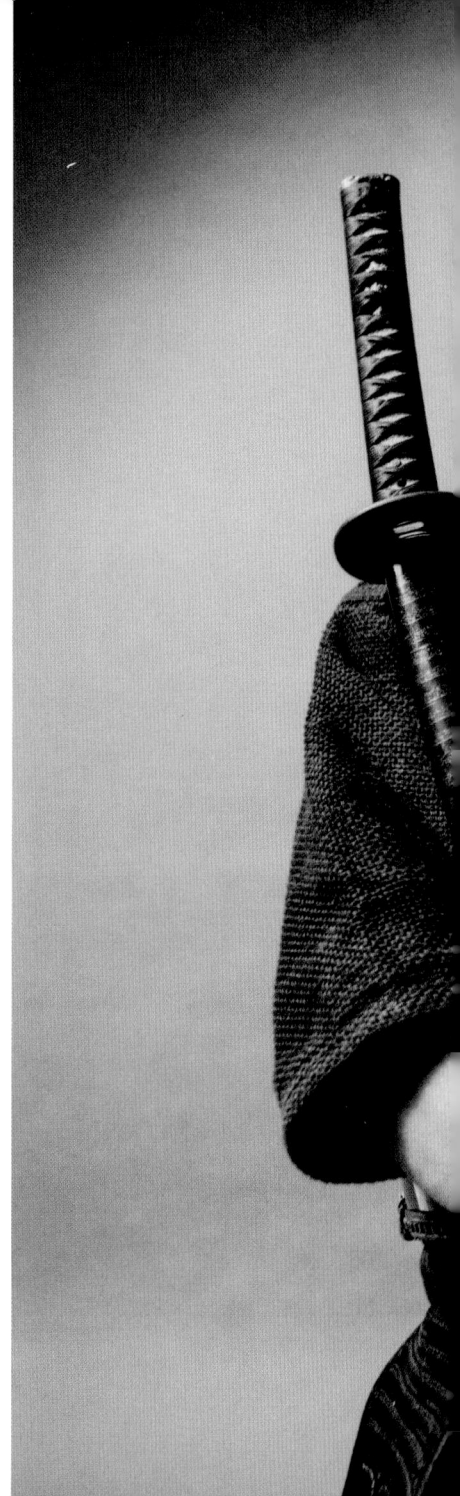

Okimitsu Fujii
2 August 1968

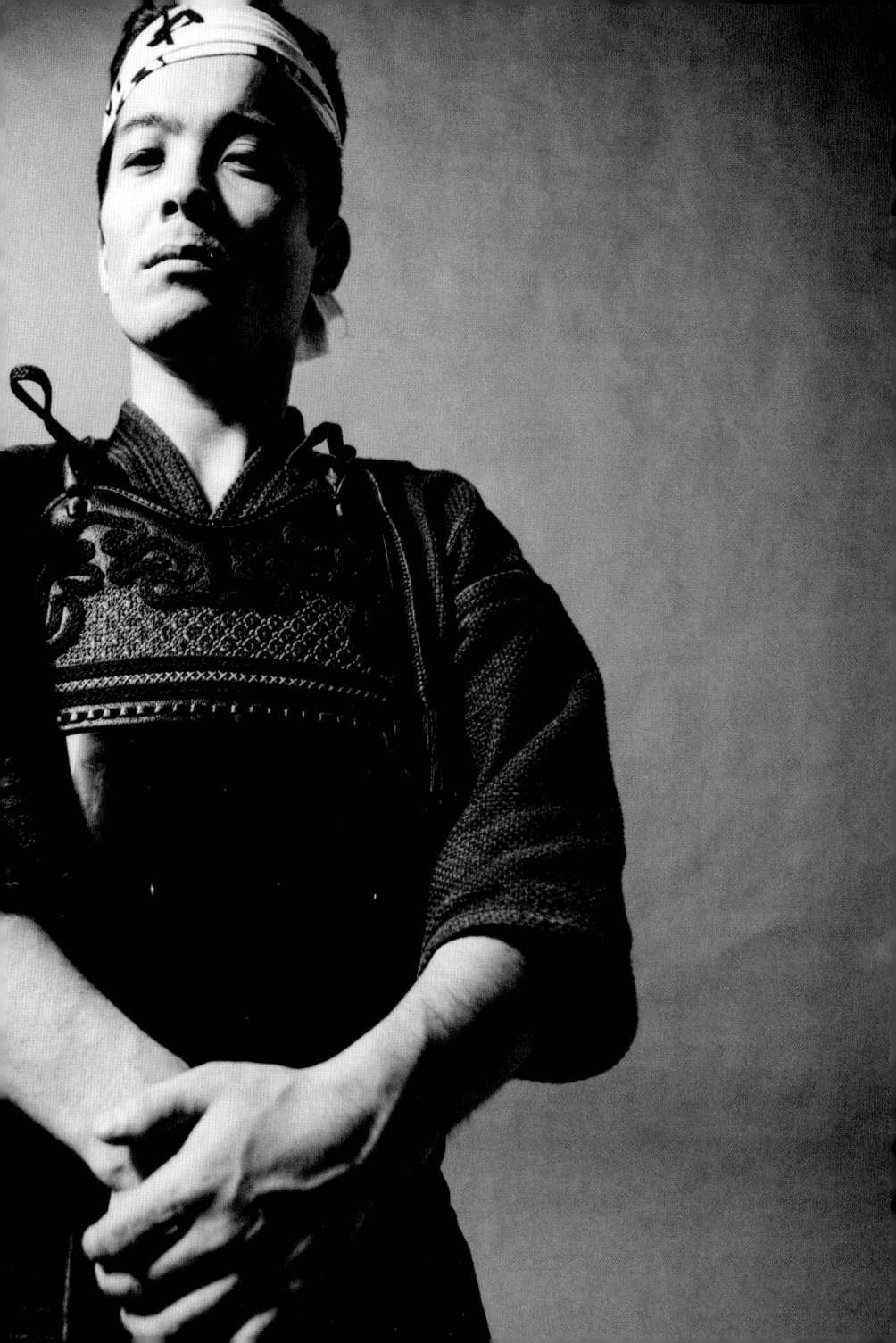

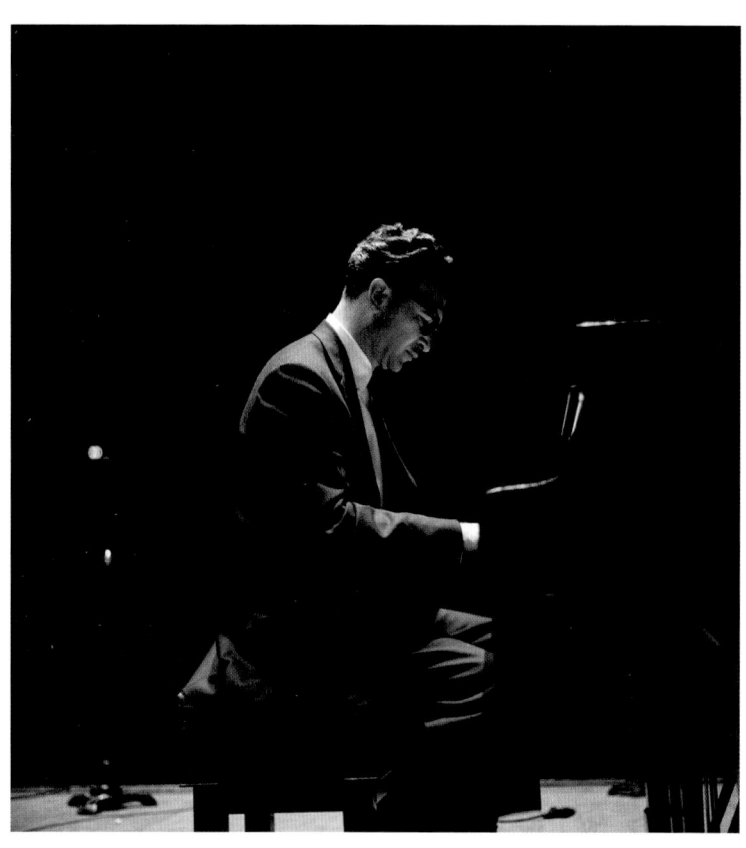

Dave Brubeck
20 March 1959

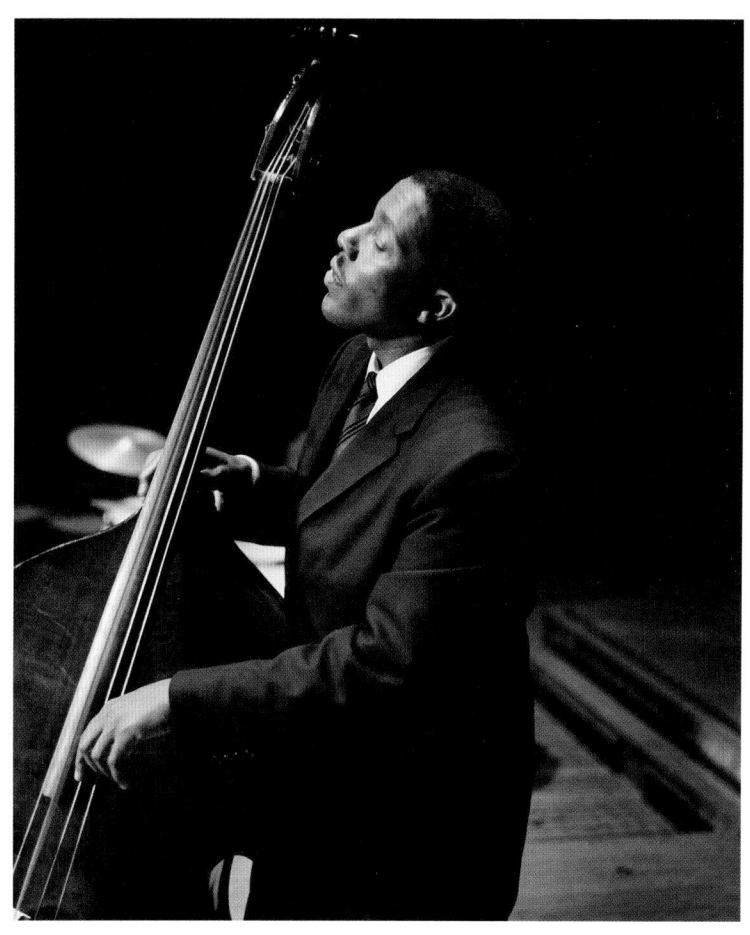

Eugene Wright
20 March 1959

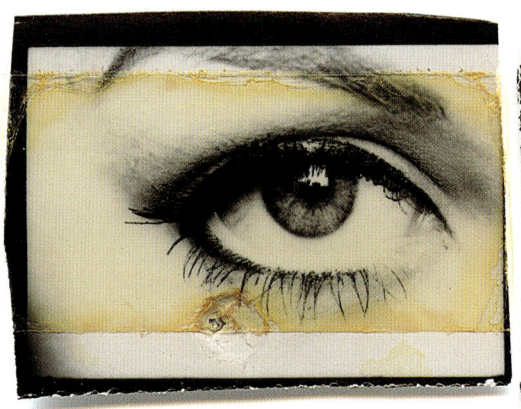
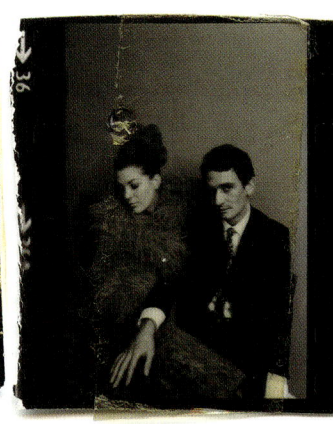
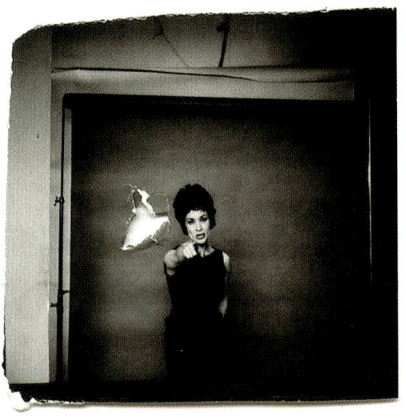
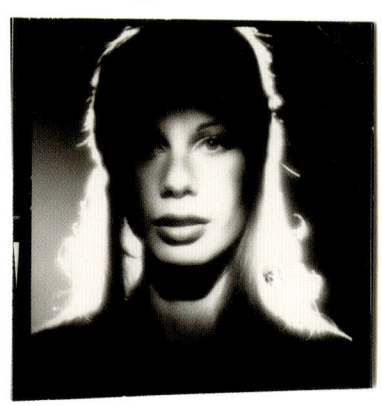
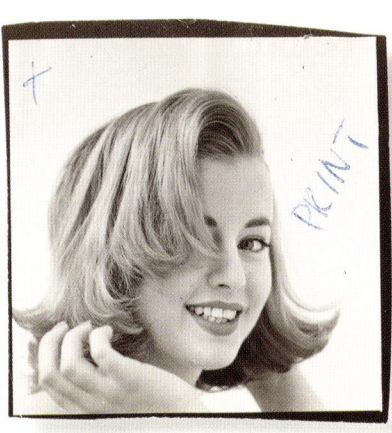
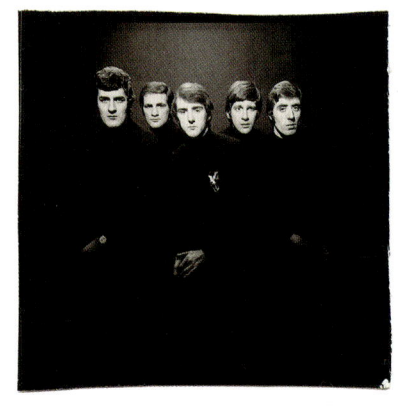

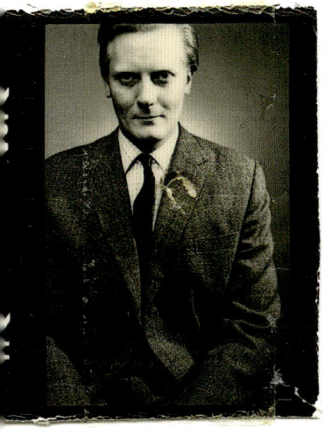

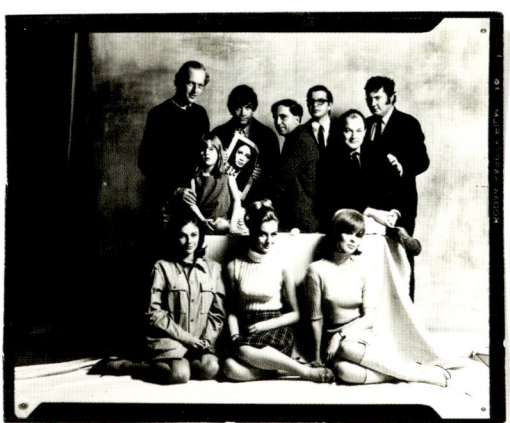

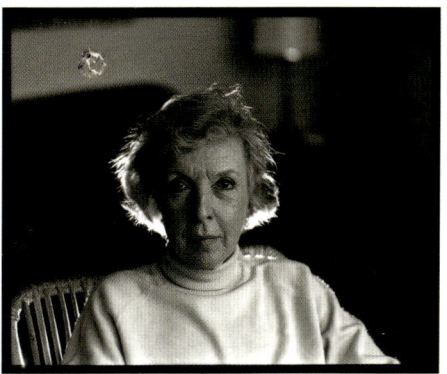

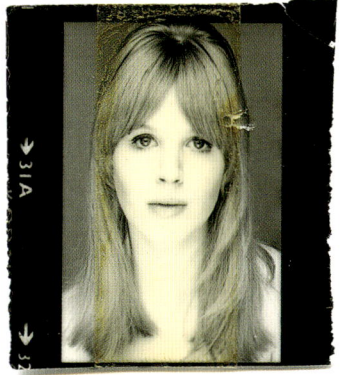

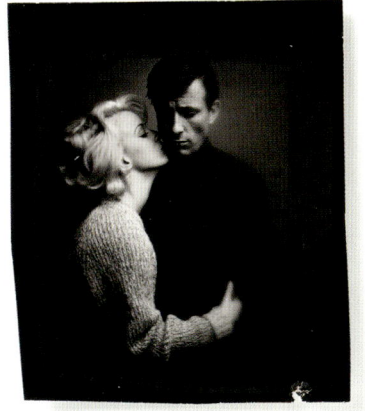

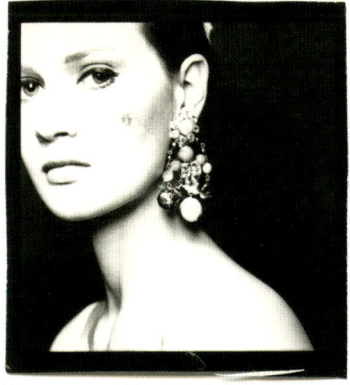

See pages 110–111 for captions

Jill Kennington
Daily Express
27 October 1966

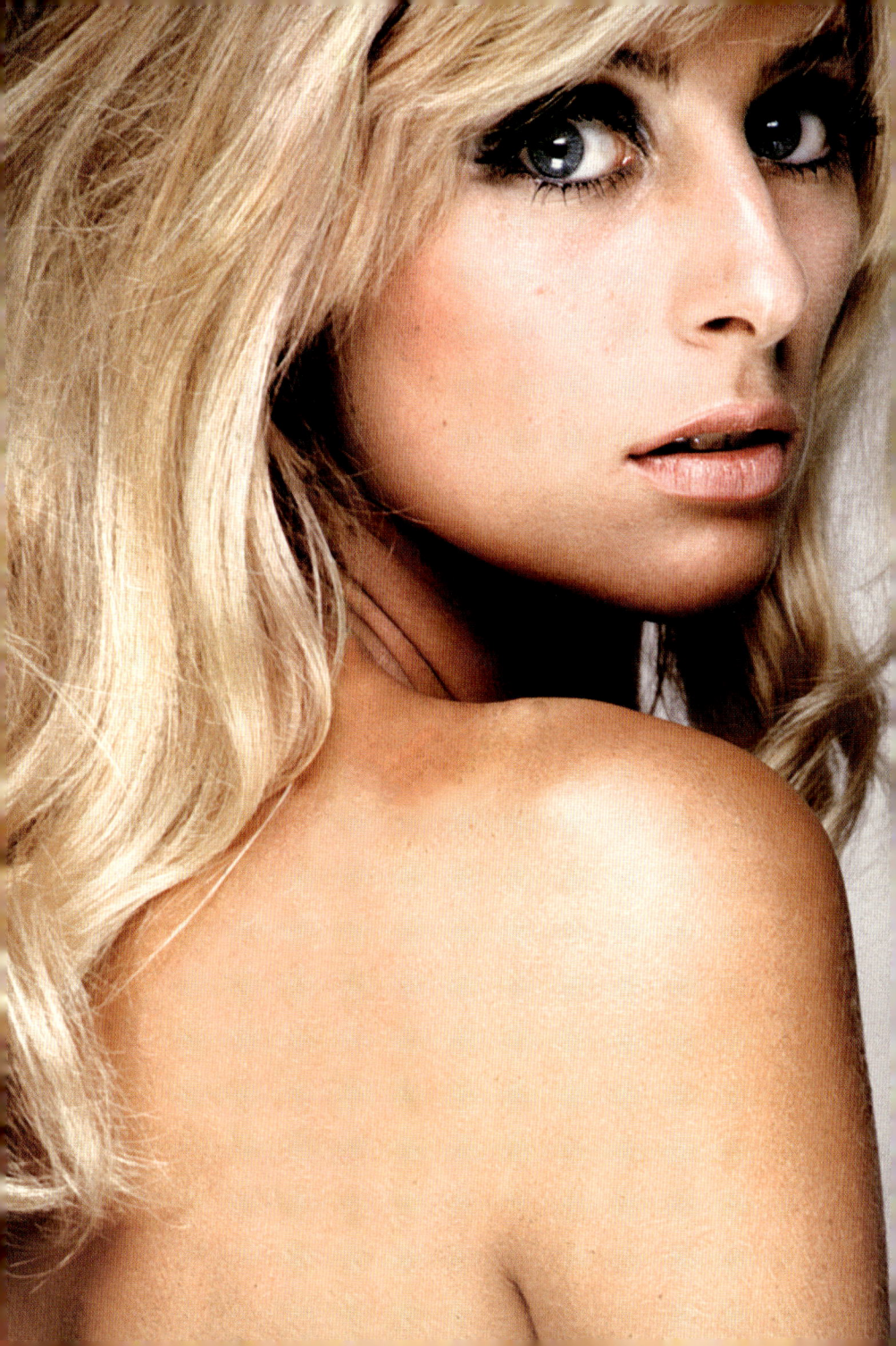

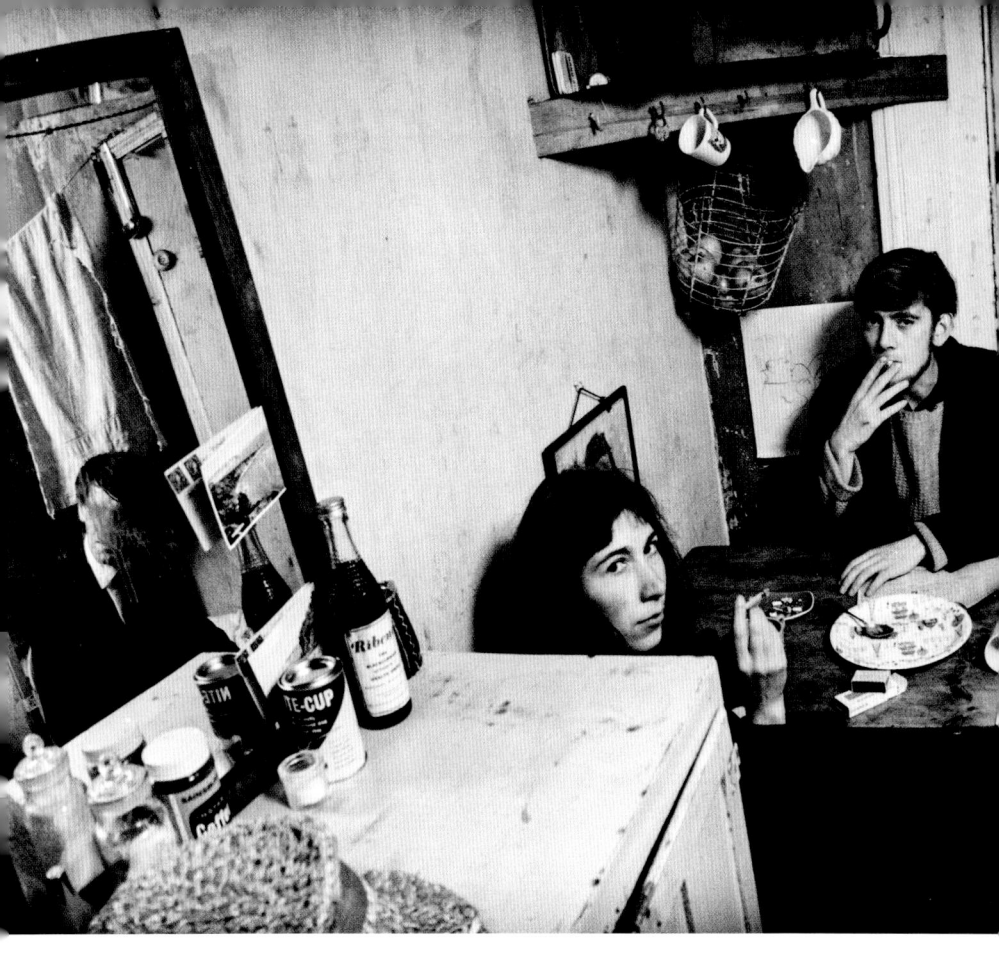

The Lay About Life
Notting Hill
Man about Town
December 1960

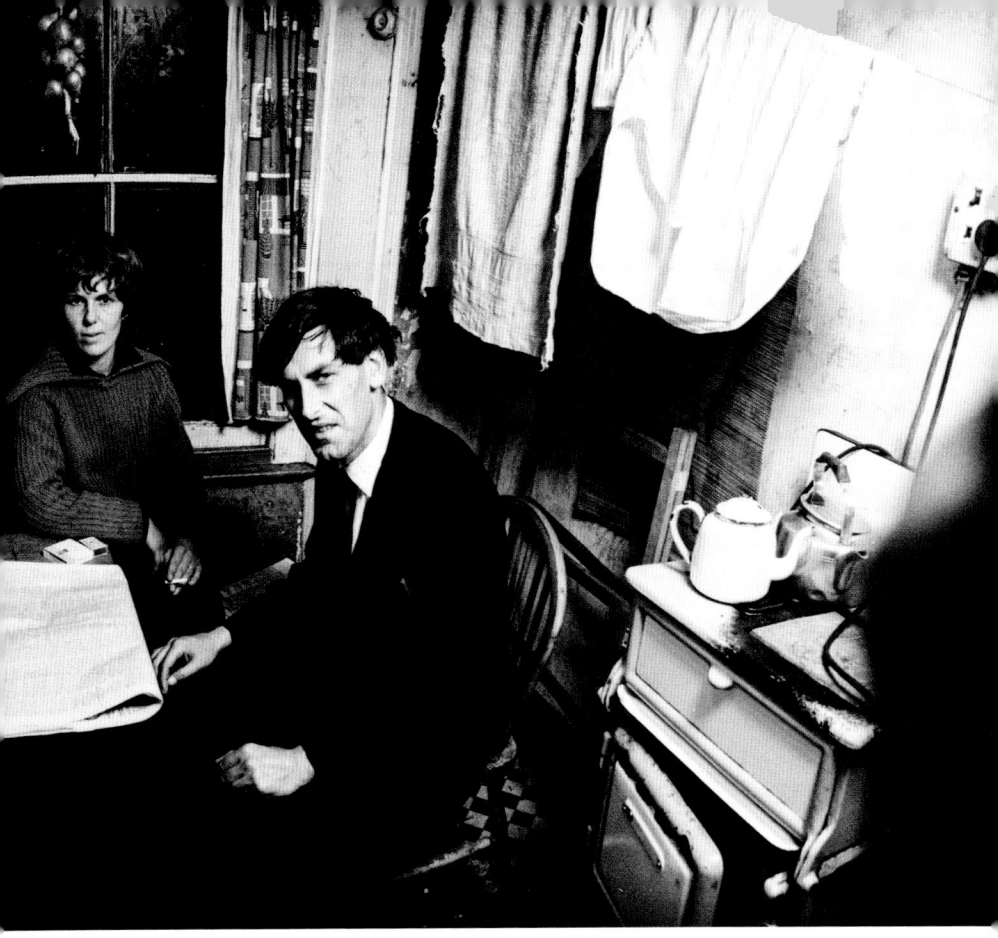

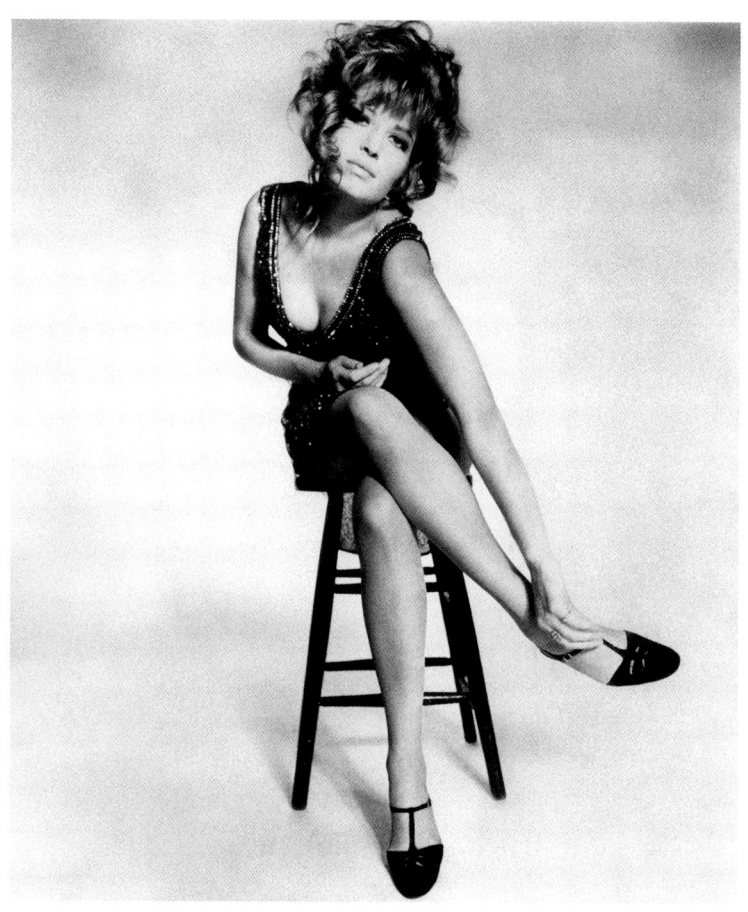

Monica Vitti
October 1967

Right
Mary Quant
18 July 1963

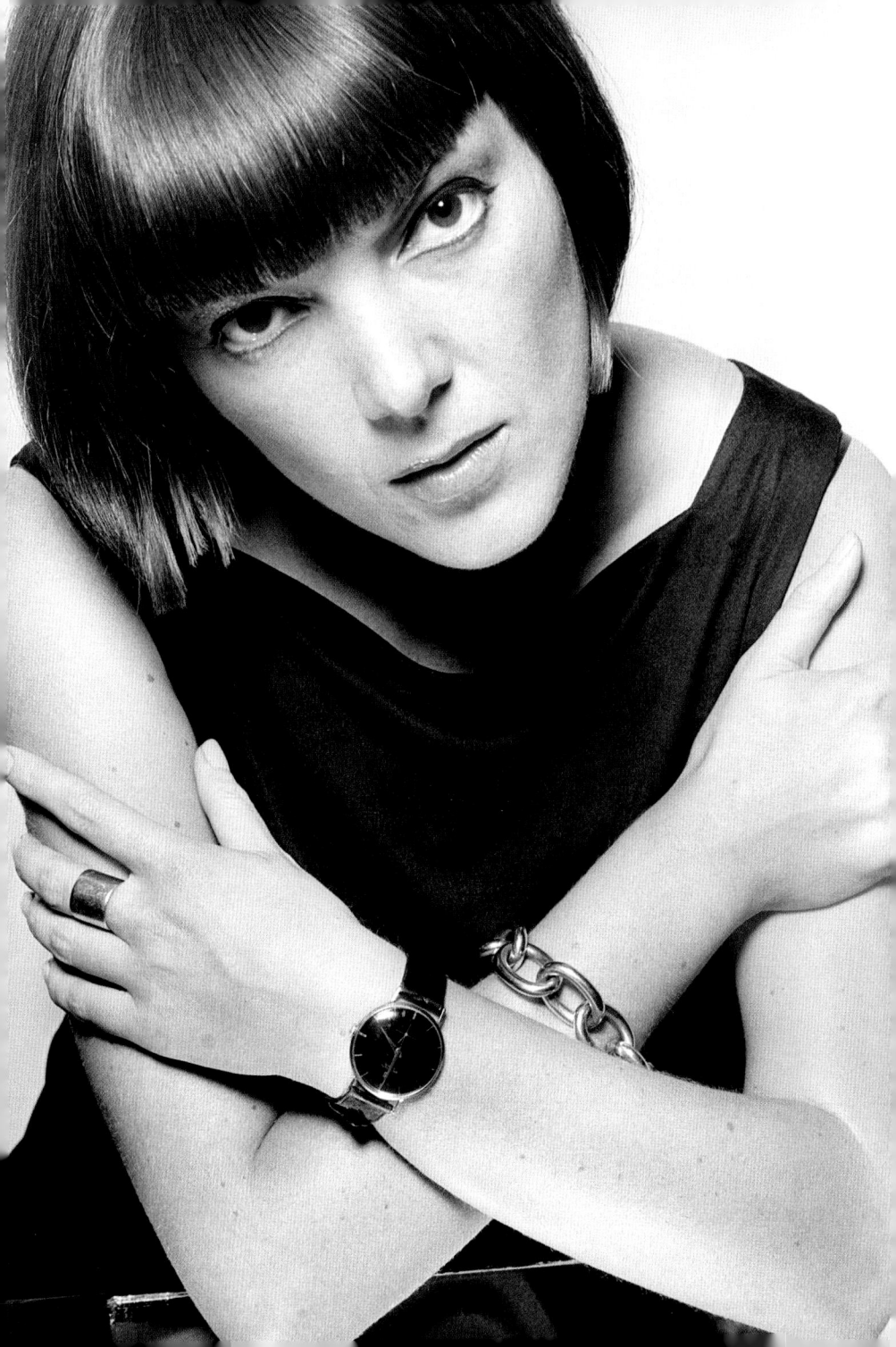

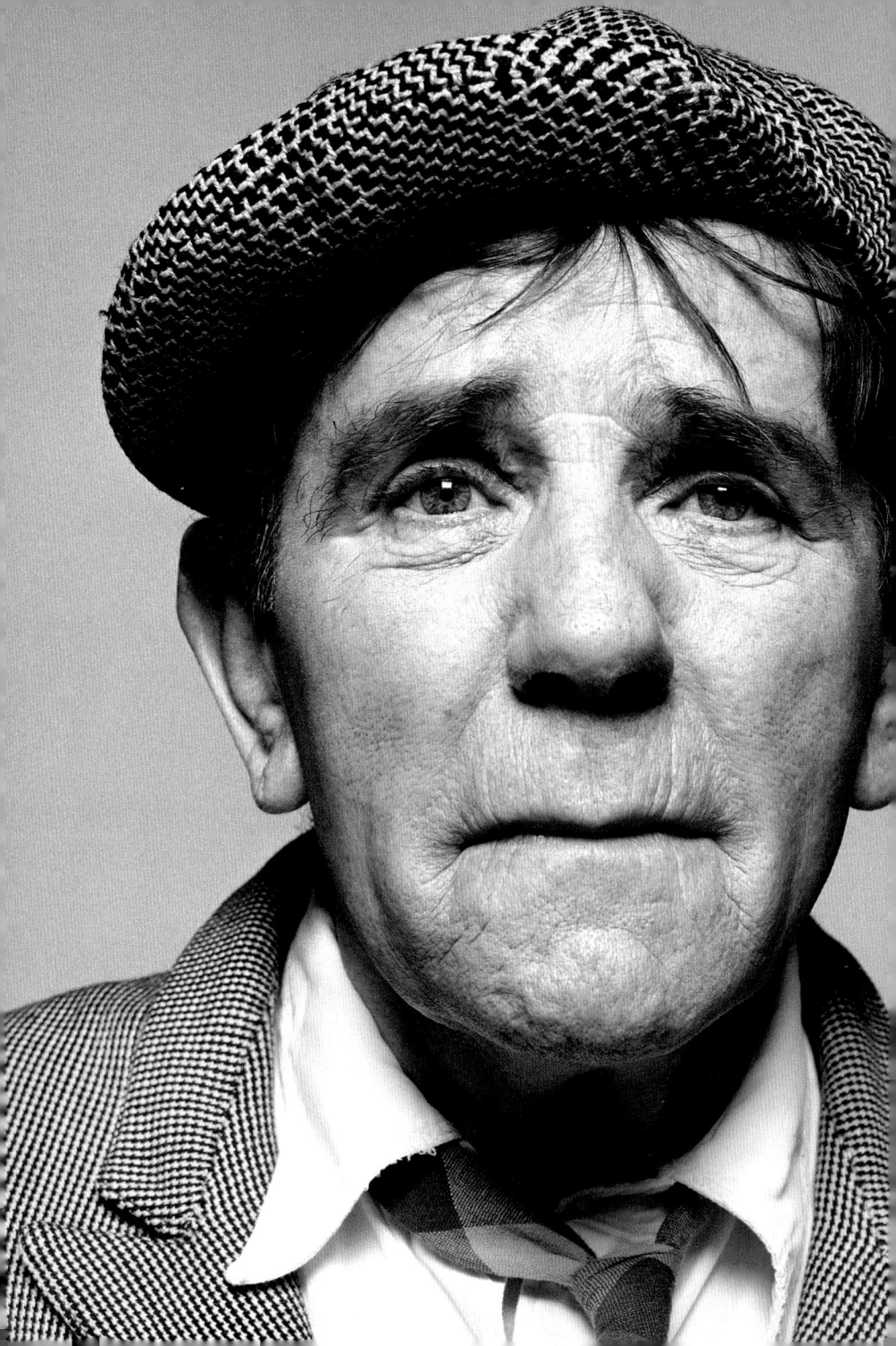

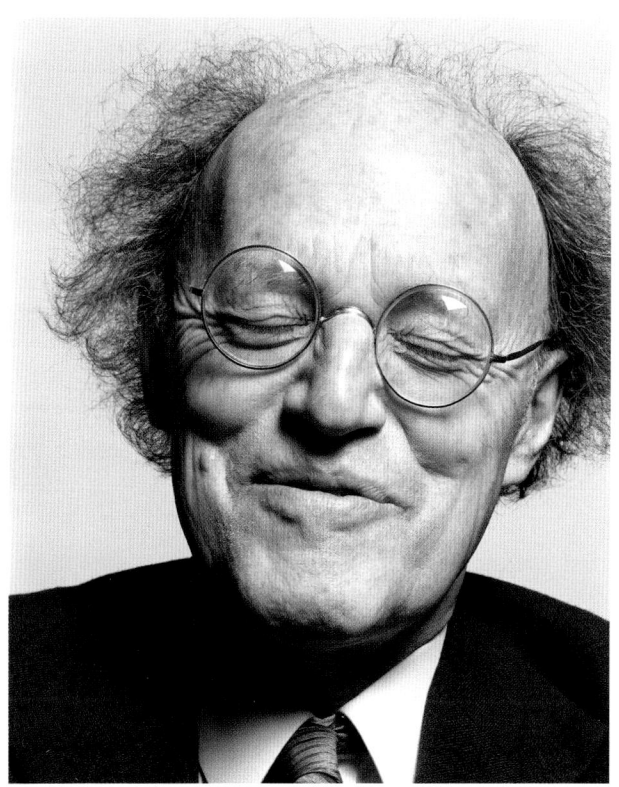

Francis Pakenham,
7th Earl of Longford
12 January 1976

Left
Norman Wisdom
British Telecom advertisement
5 October 1988

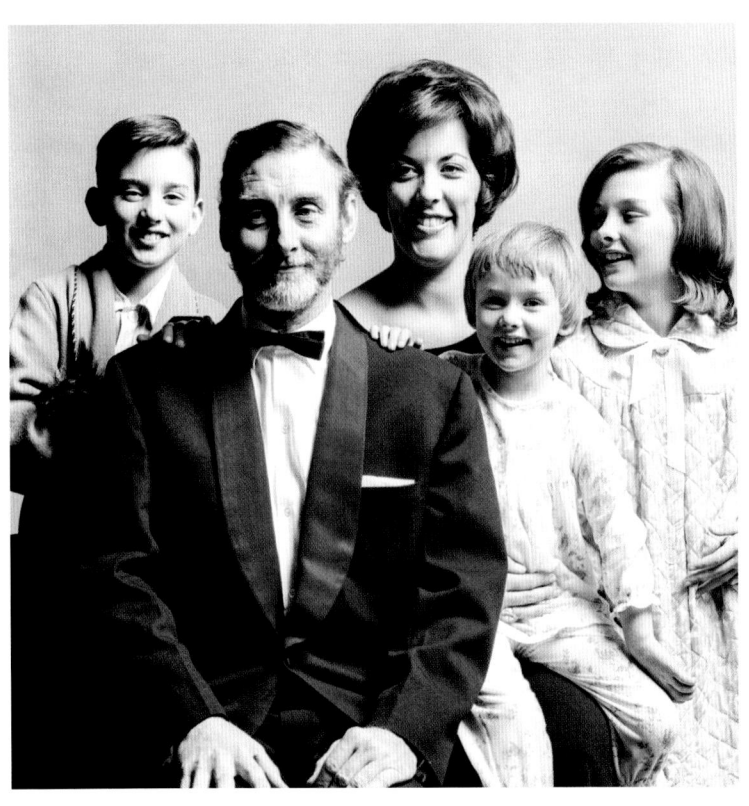

Spike Milligan and his family
Harper's Bazaar
1 October 1963

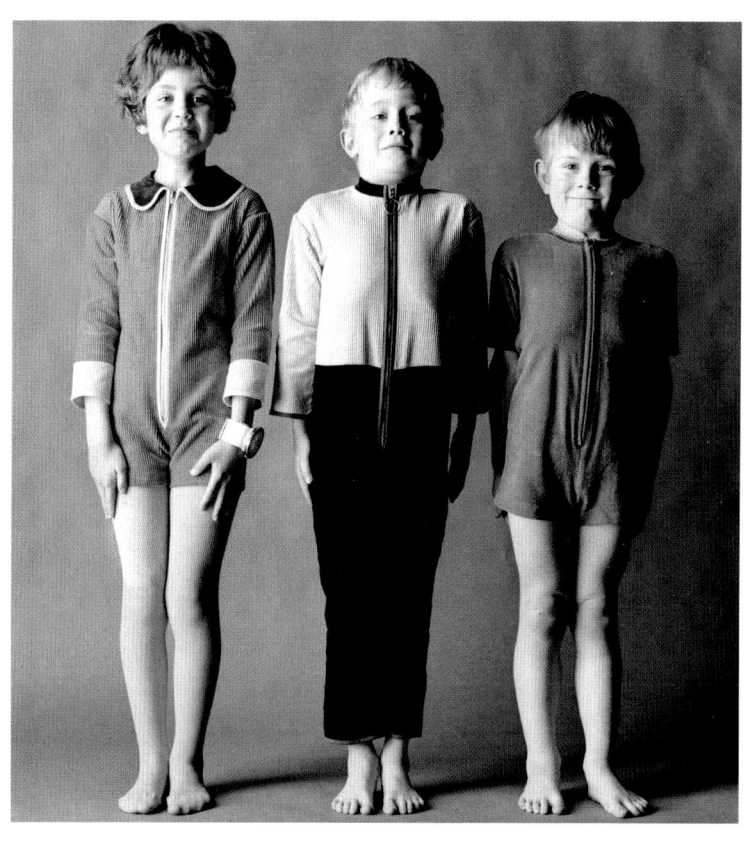

Julian Brand, Dominic Brand
and John Foster
April 1967

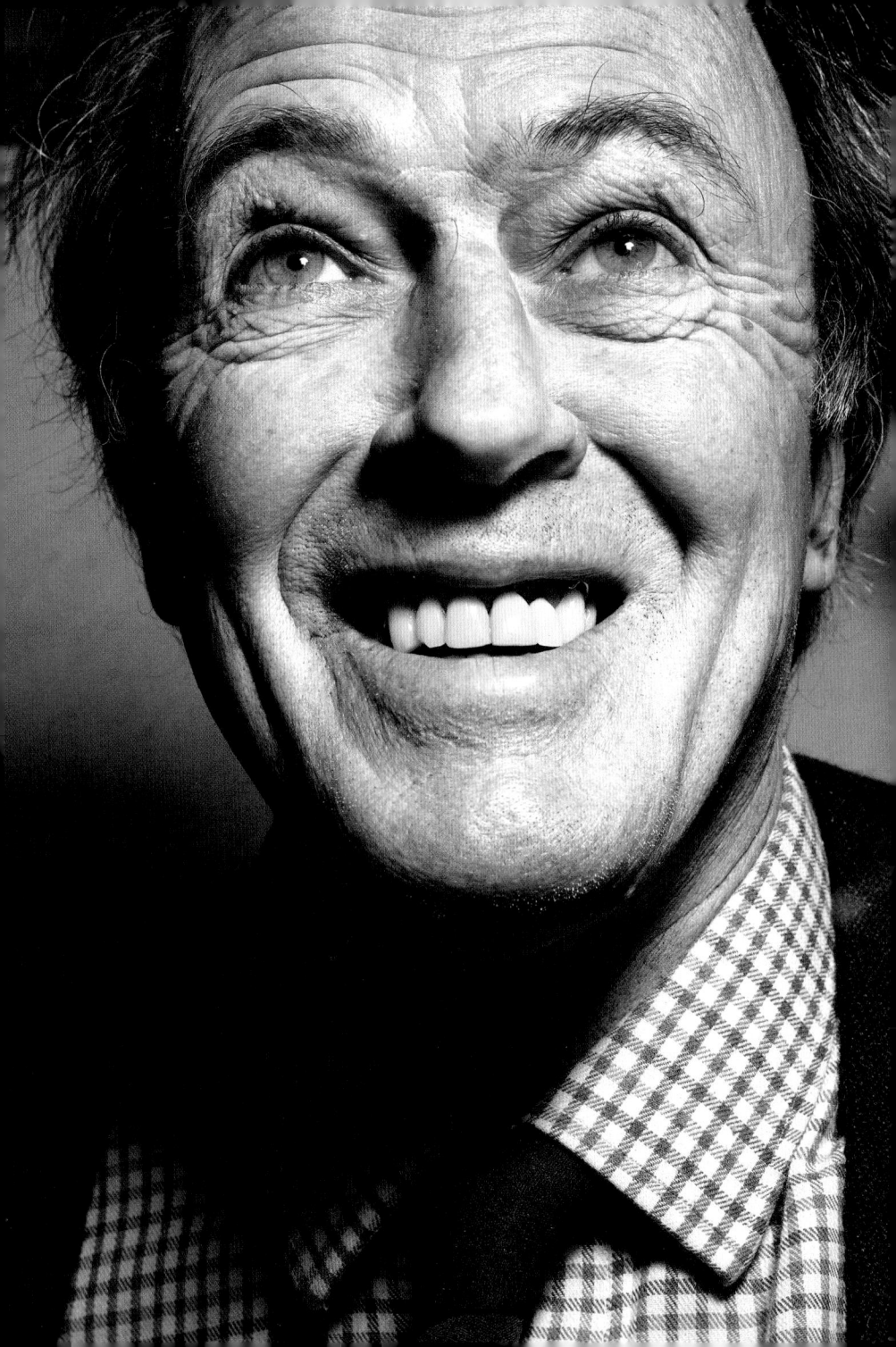

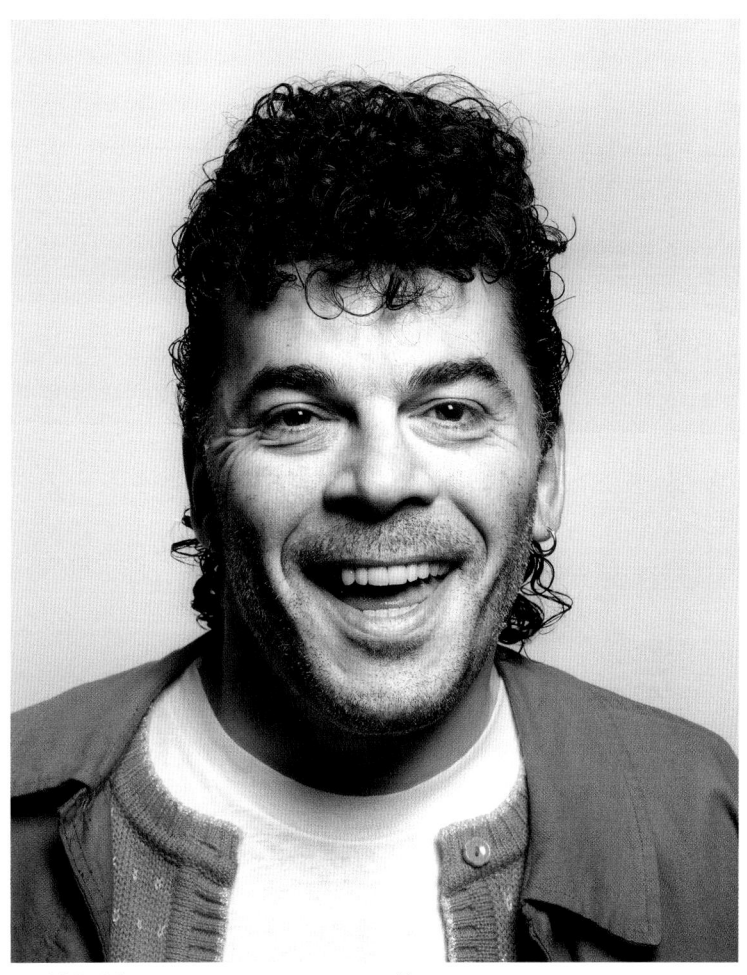

Roald Dahl
British *Vogue*
February 1979

Above
Ian Dury
1981

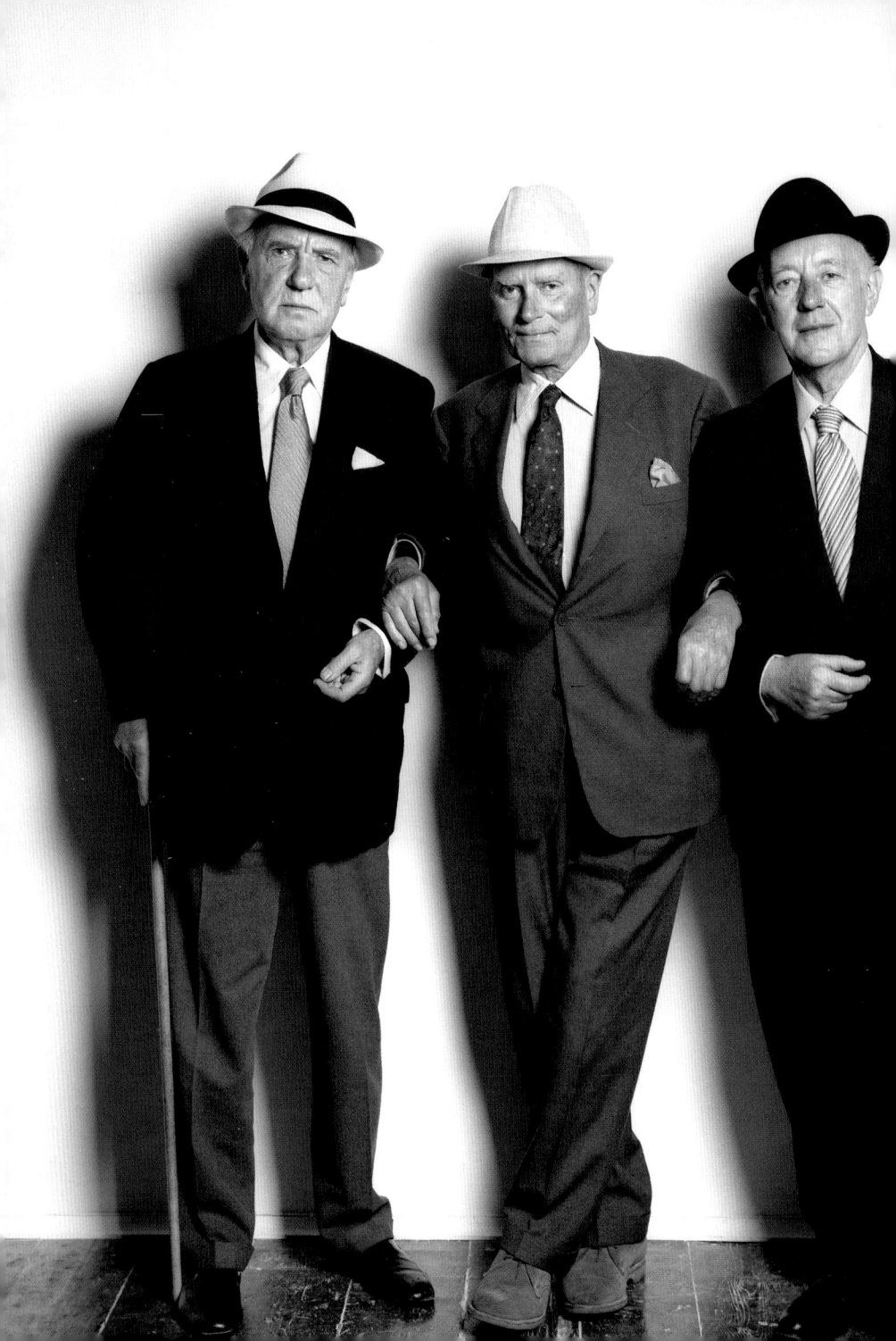

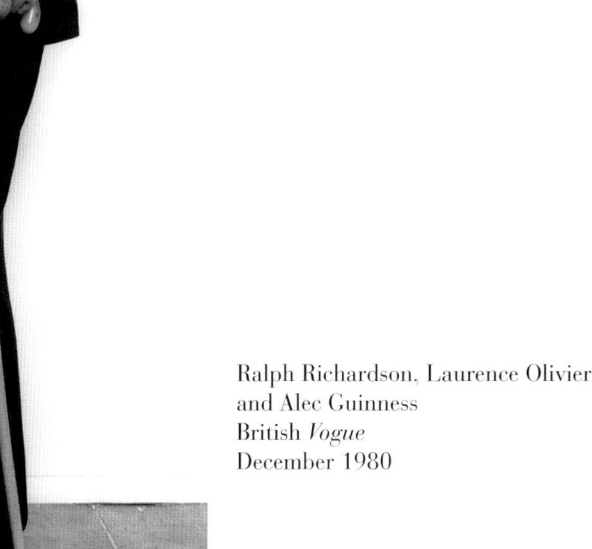

Ralph Richardson, Laurence Olivier
and Alec Guinness
British *Vogue*
December 1980

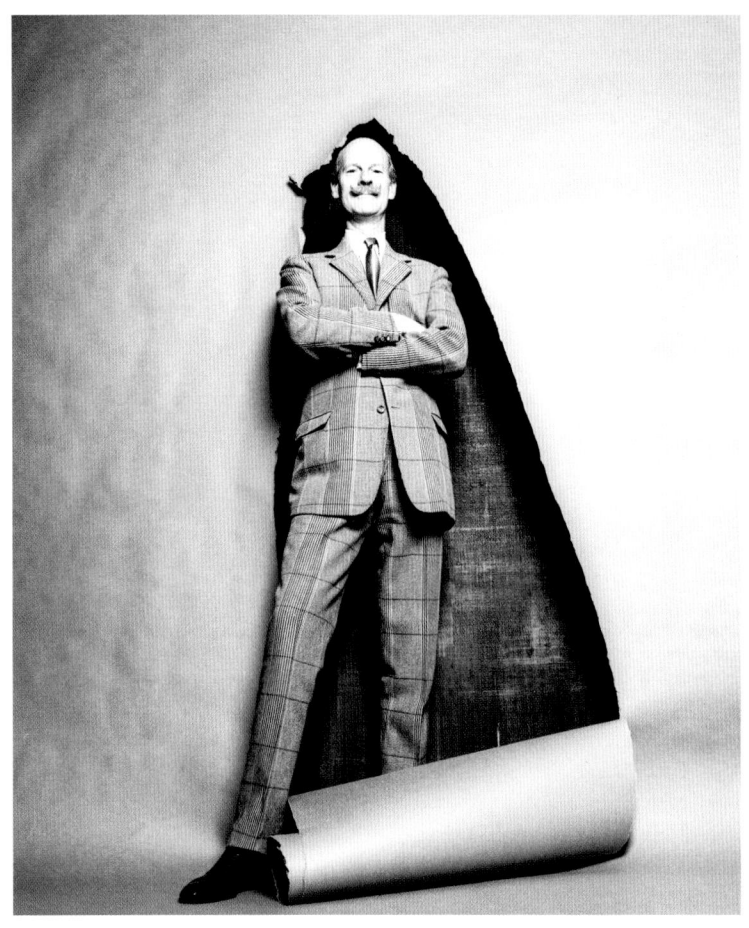

Norman Parkinson
Sunday Times
22 December 1960

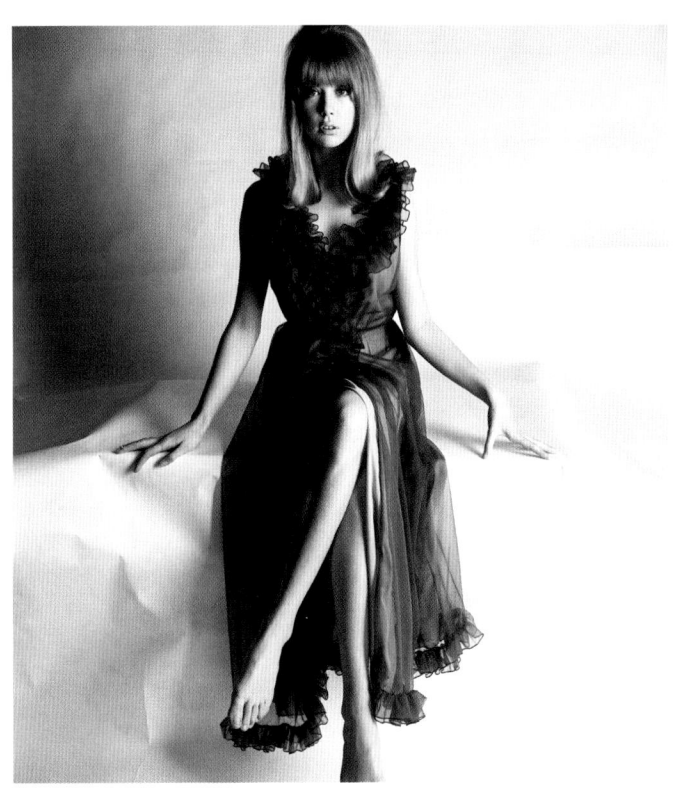

Pattie Boyd
Sunday Mirror
20 November 1964

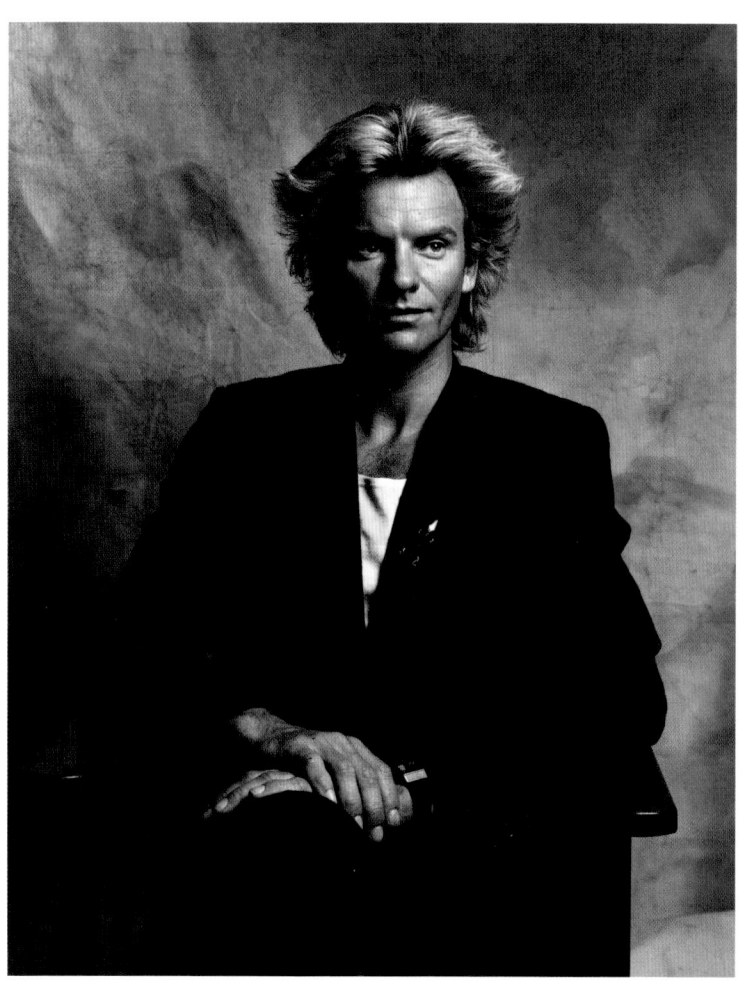

Sting
British *Vogue*
1984

Right
Jeremy Irons
Sunday Telegraph magazine
9 July 1989

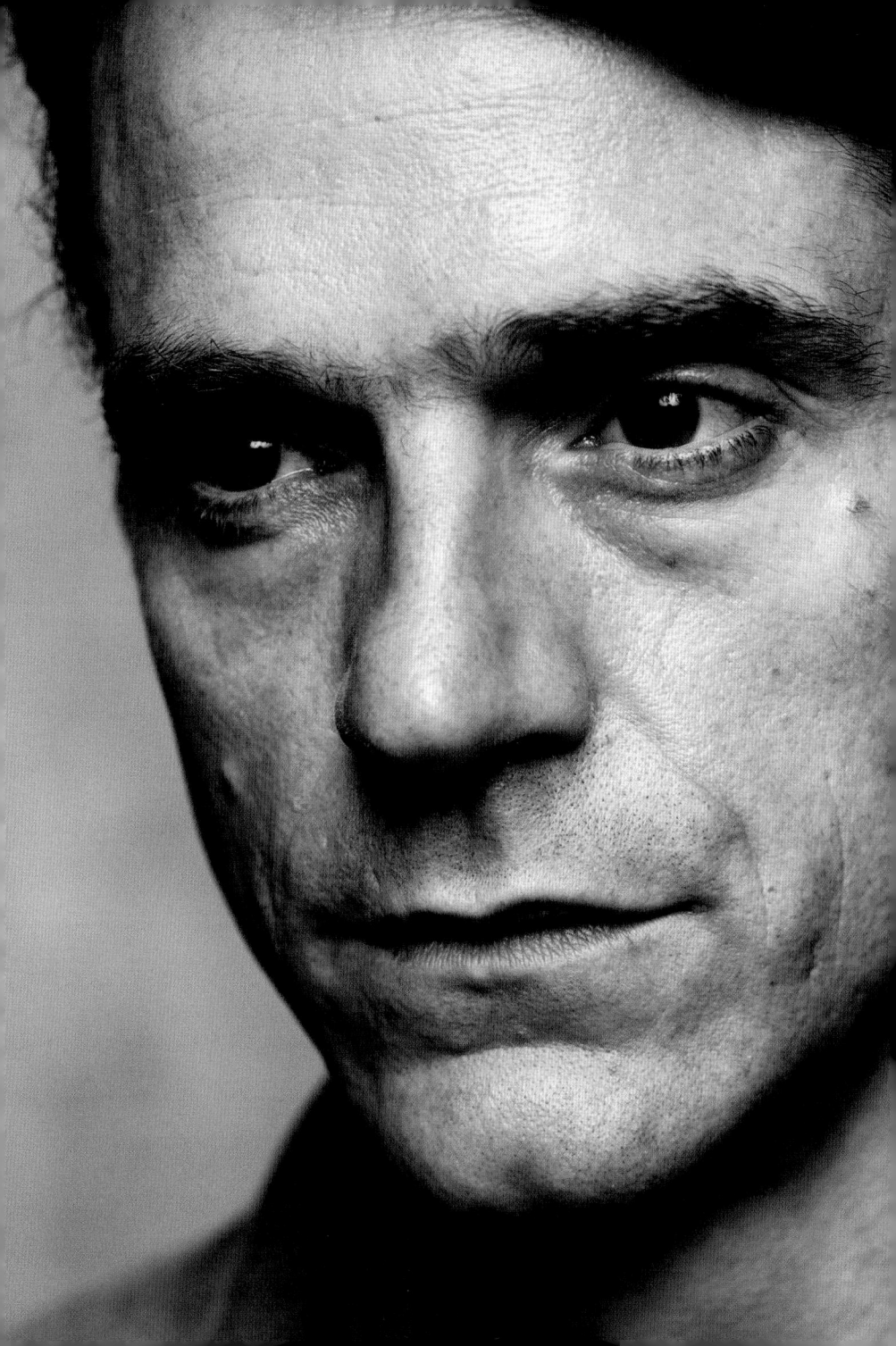

Debbie Harry
Cosmopolitan
December 1978

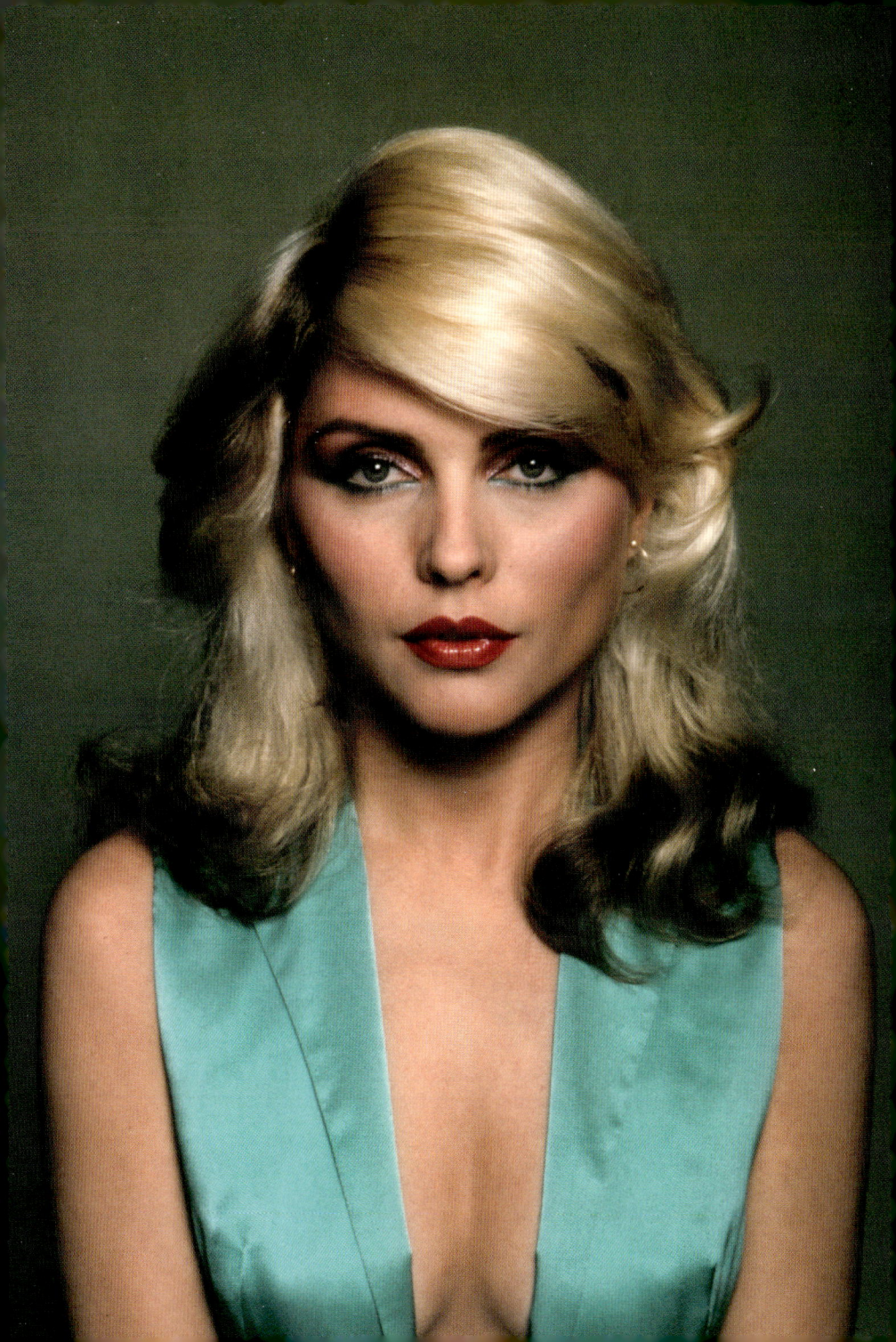

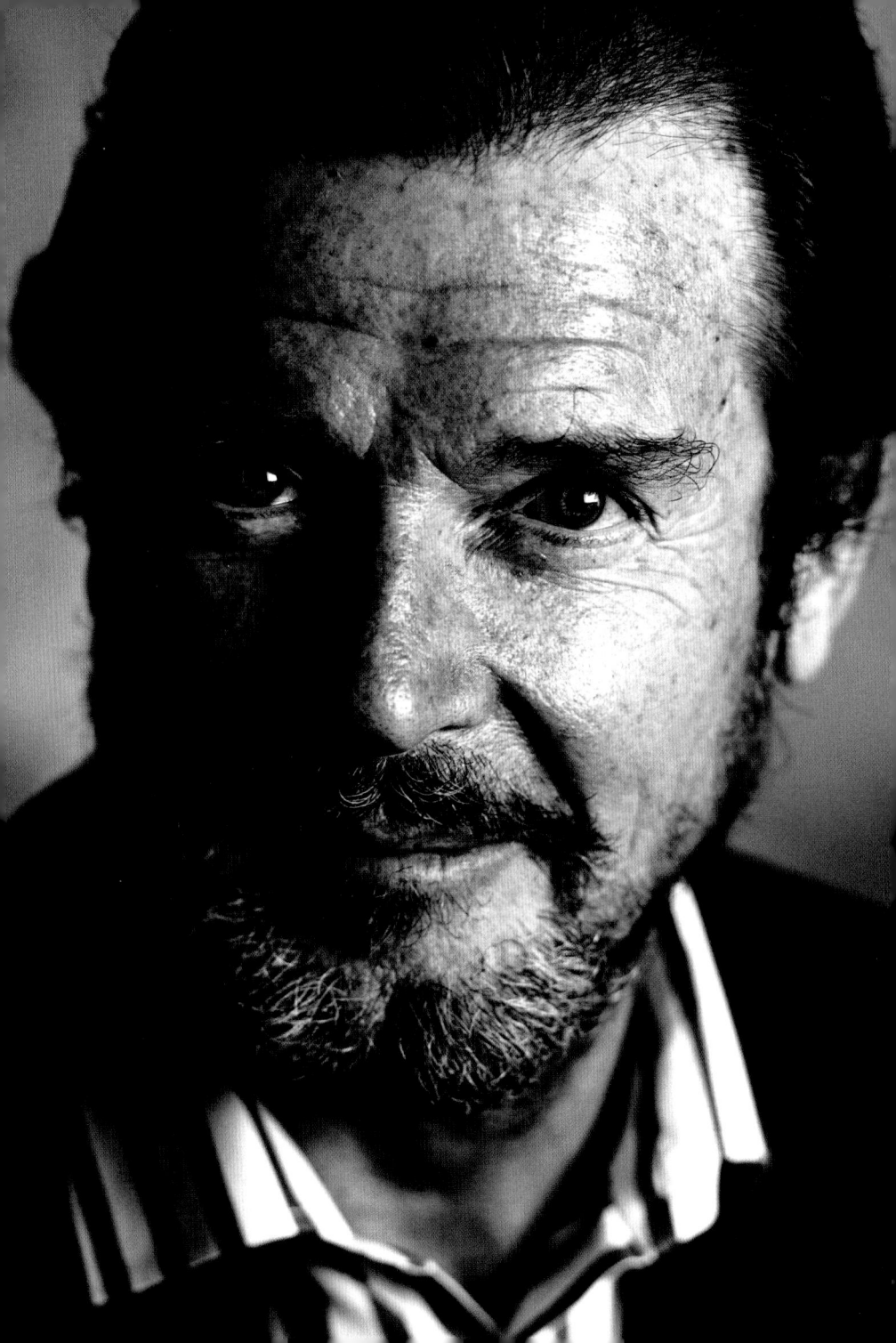

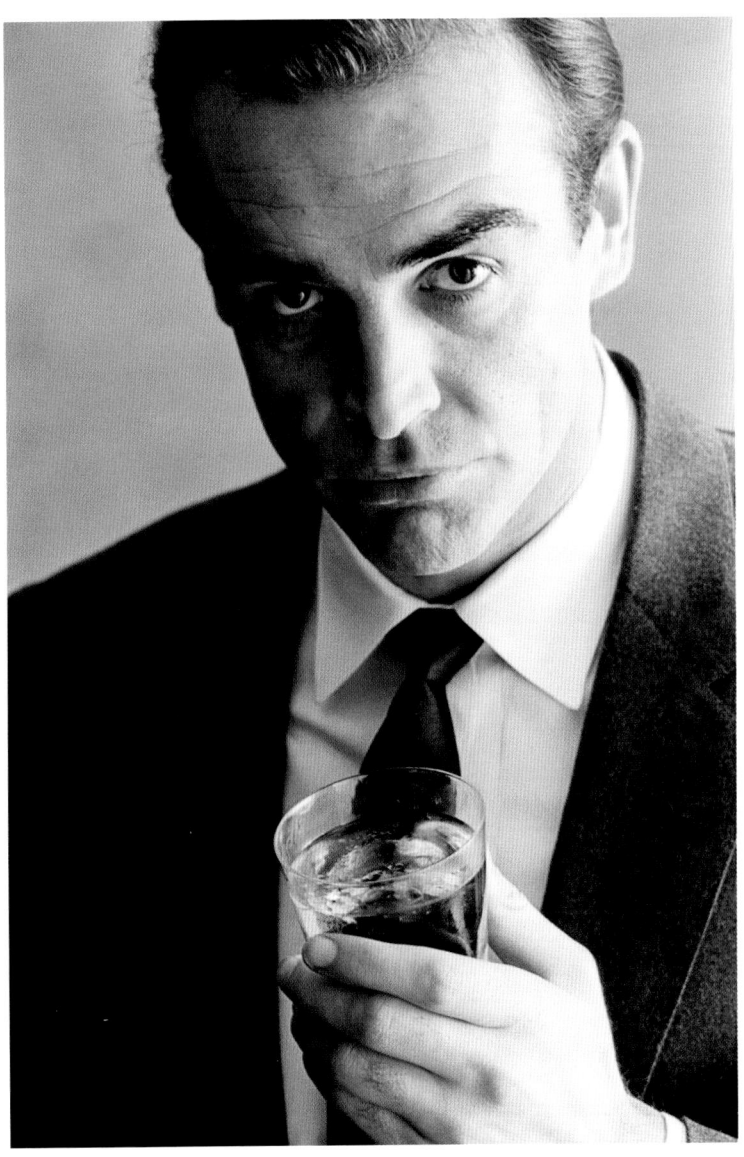

Roger Moore
23 February 1989

Above
Sean Connery
1 January 1962

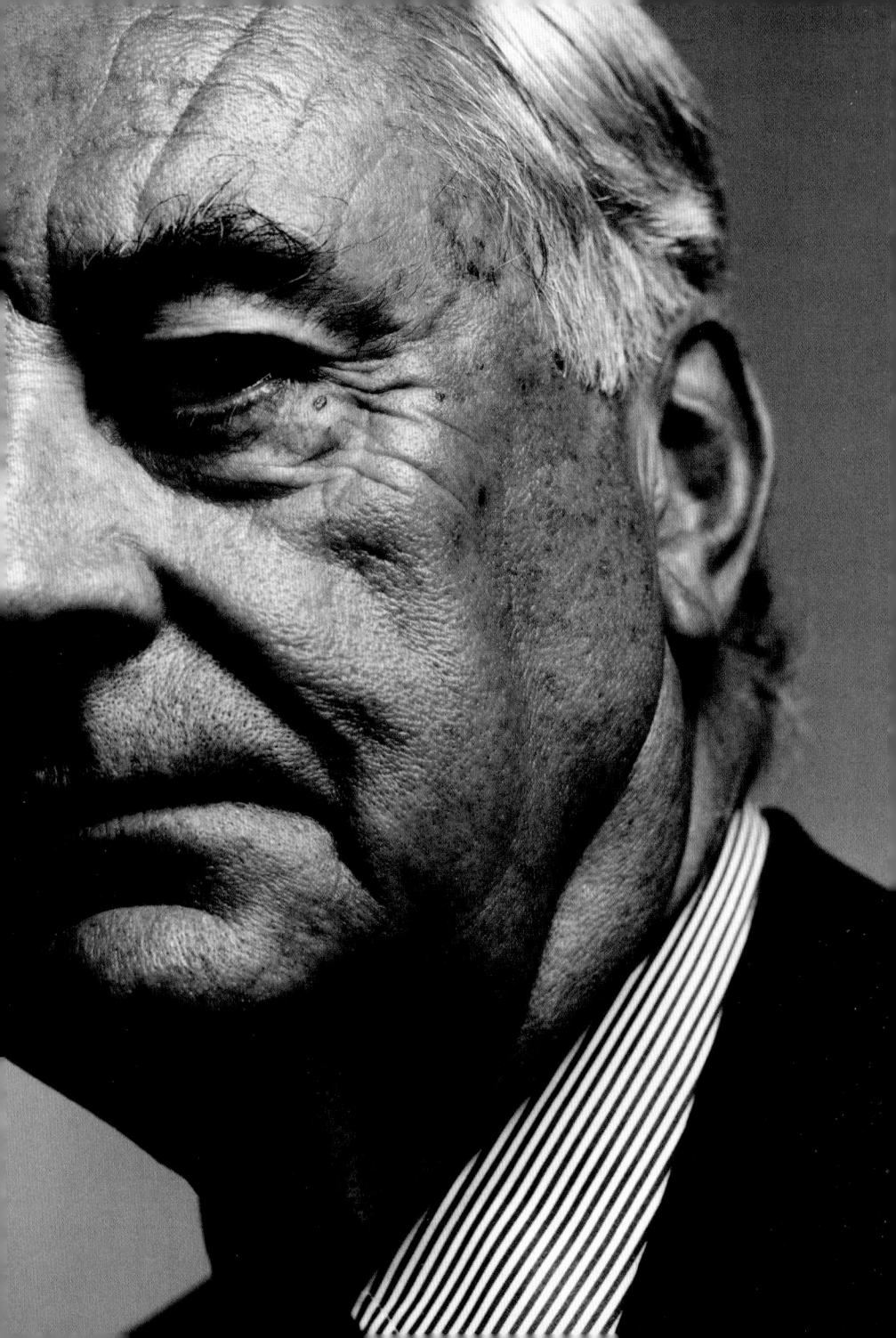

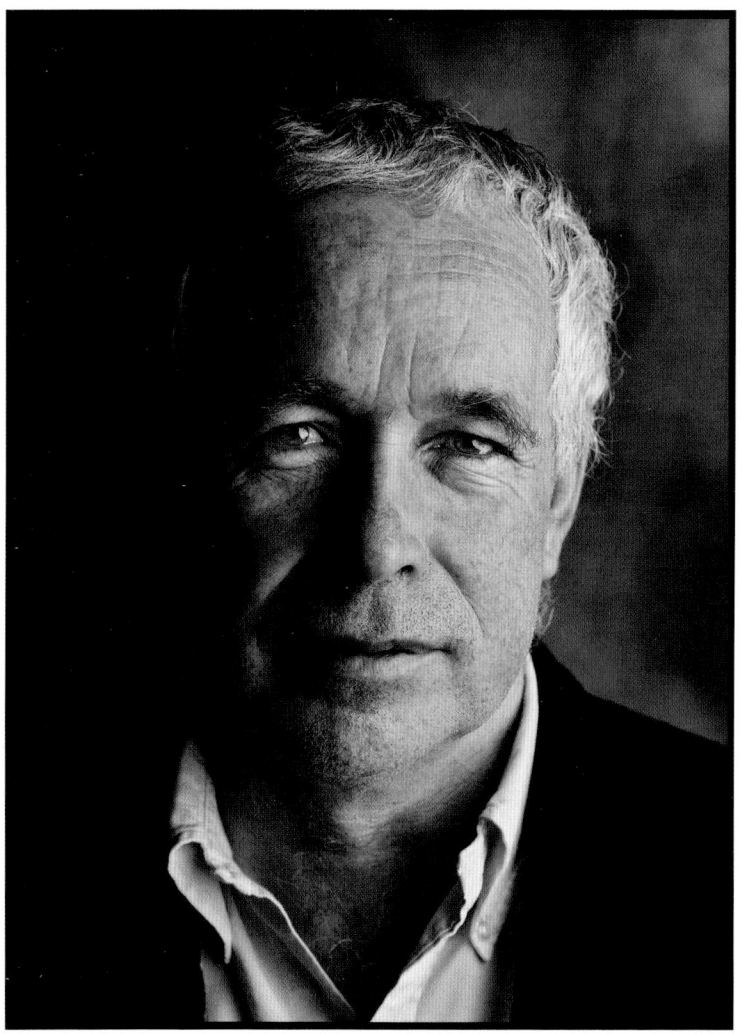

Mark Birley
19 June 1996

Above
Howard Hodgkin
9 October 1990

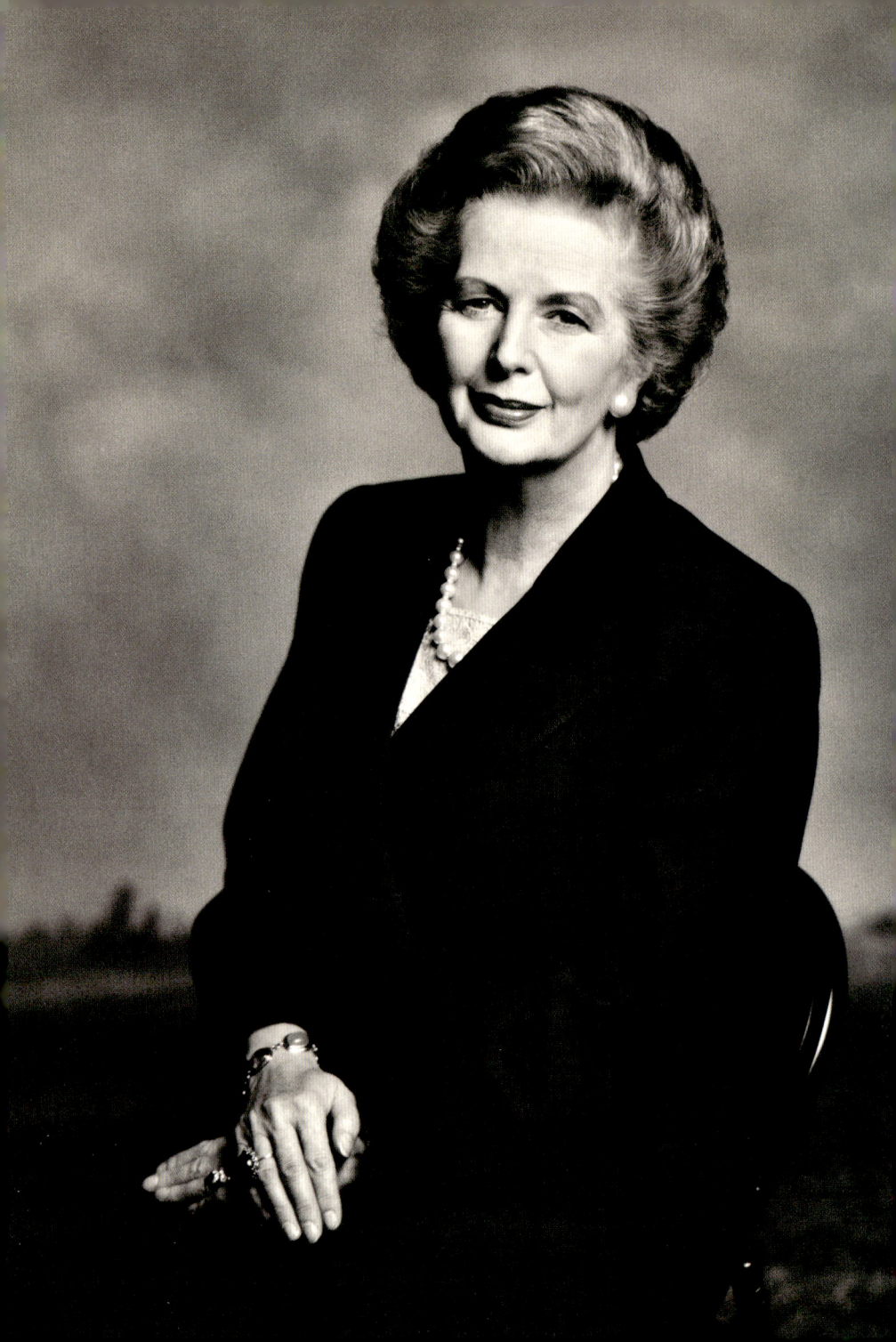

Margaret Thatcher
18 January 1991

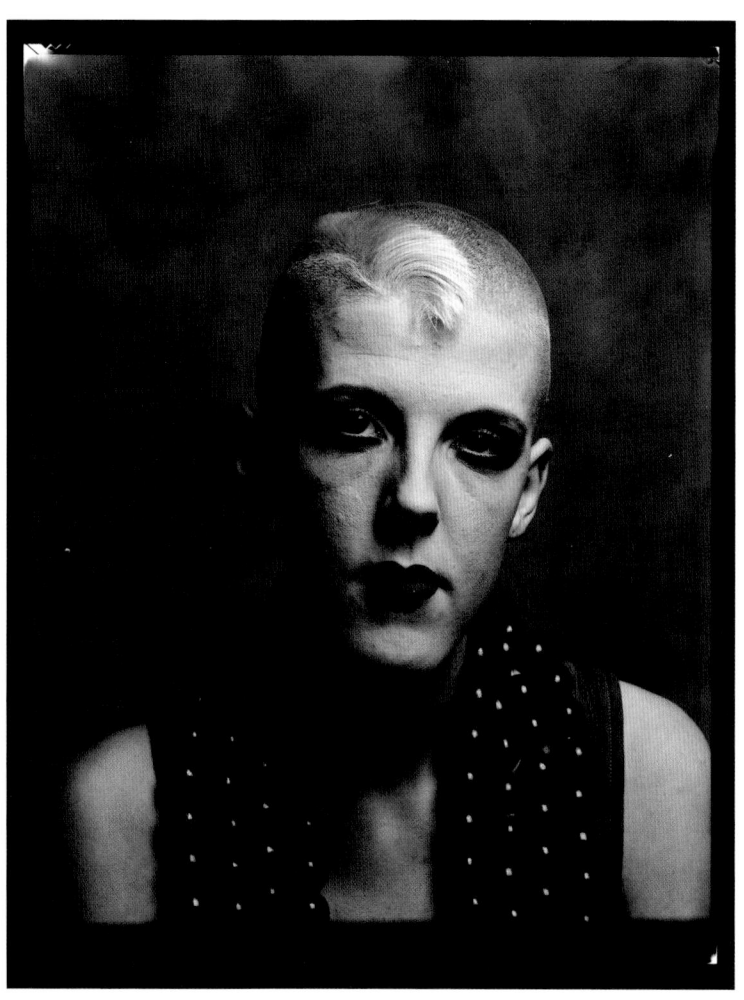

Scarlett
Femme
30 March 1984

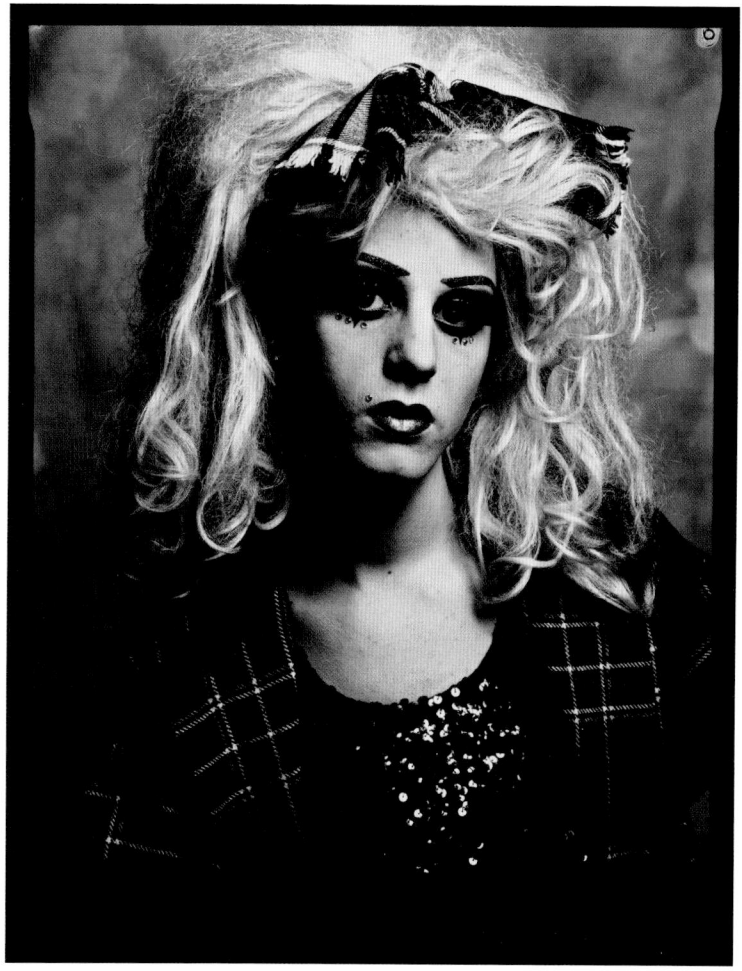

Tasty Tim
Femme
30 March 1984

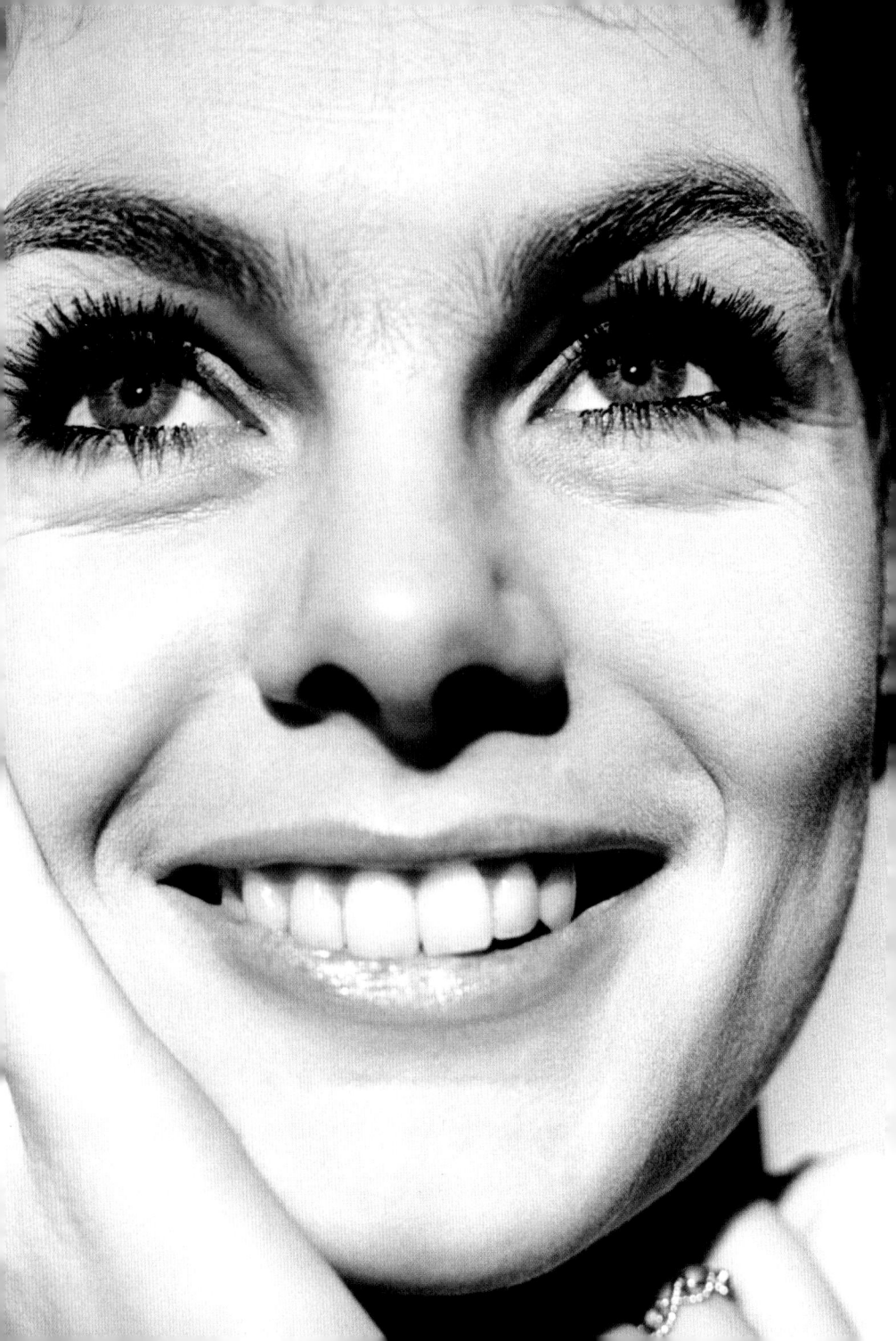

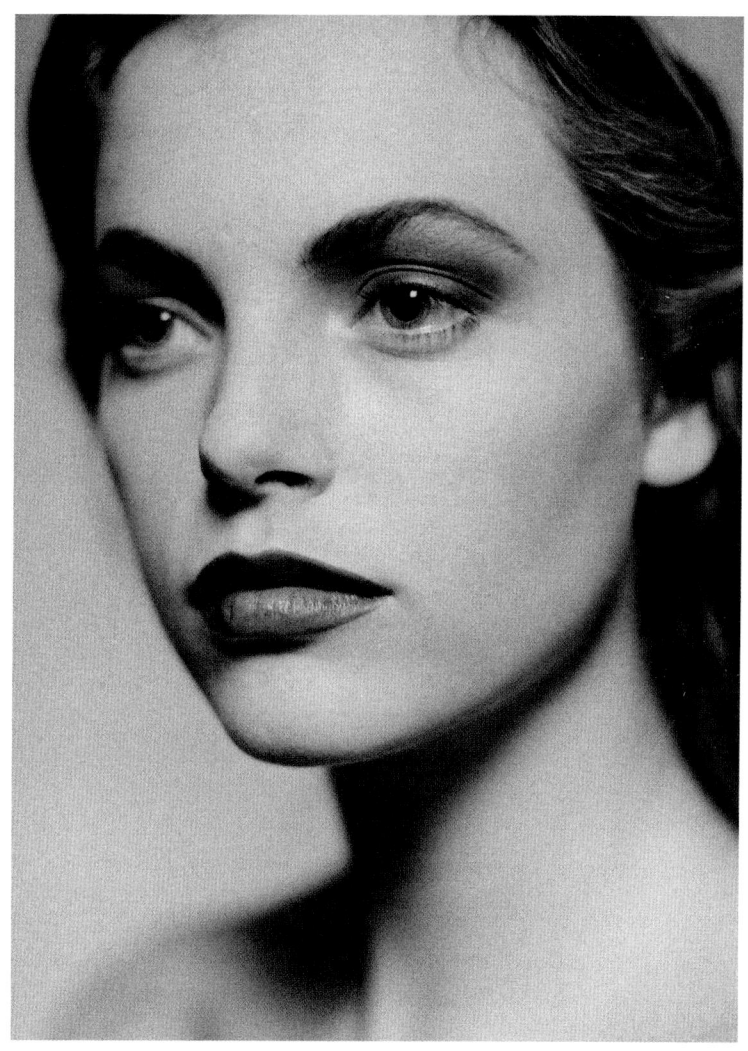

Jean Shrimpton
17 January 1967

Above
Nadia
Ritz
27 June 1989

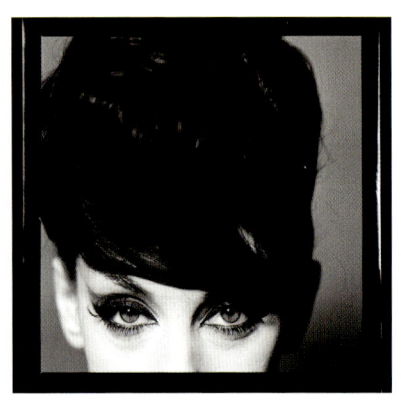
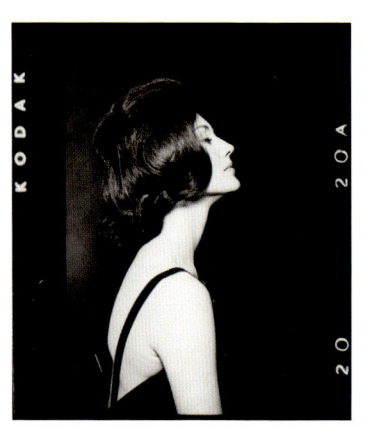
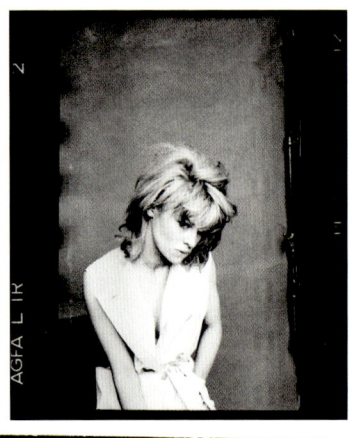
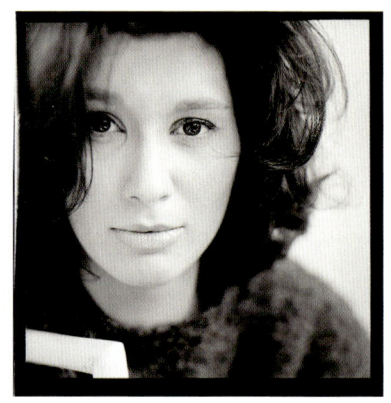
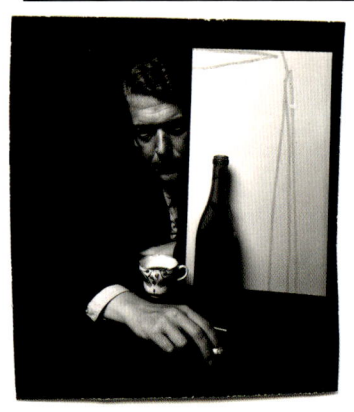
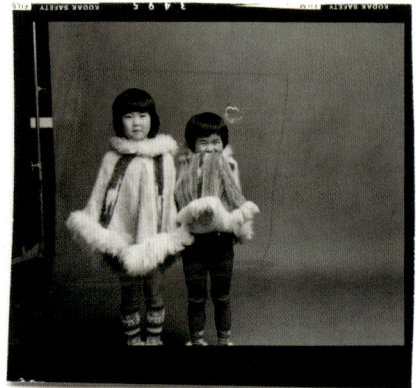

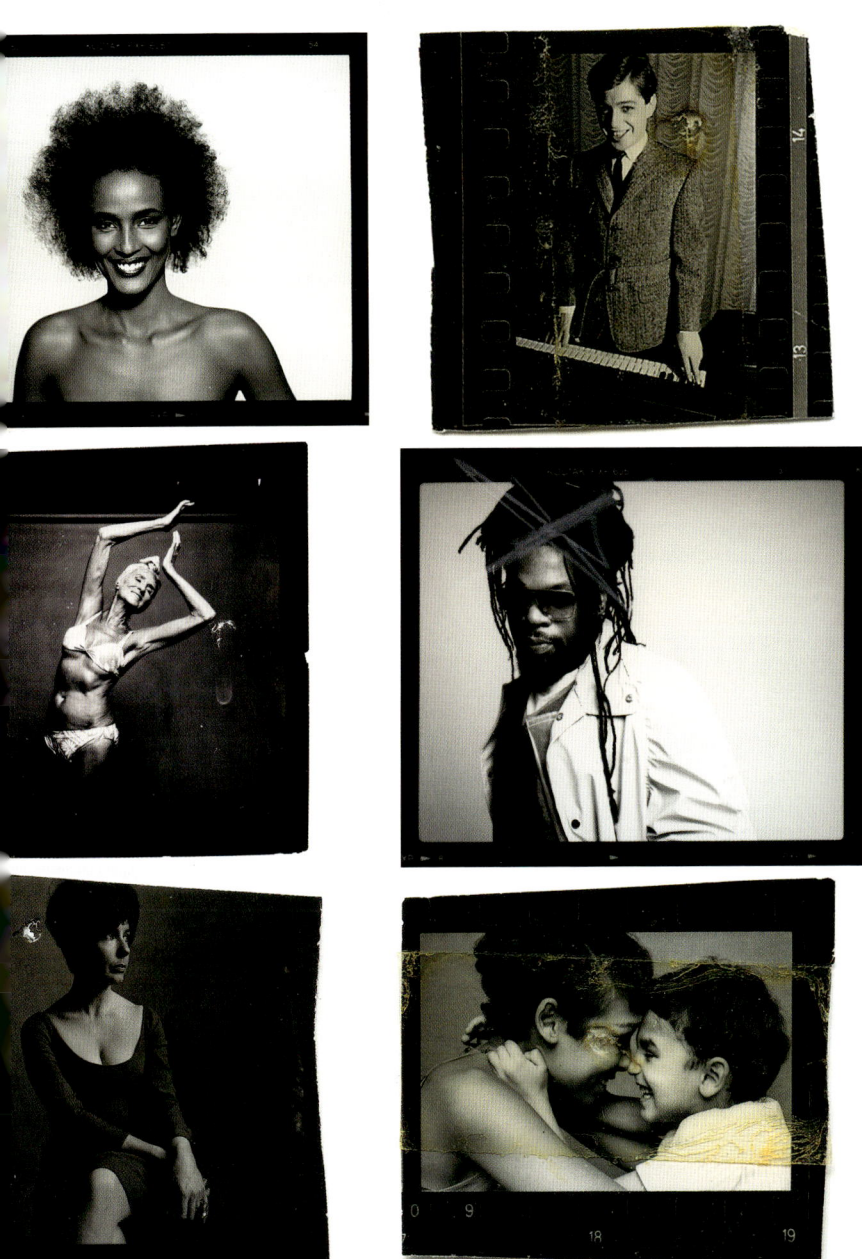

See pages 110–111 for captions

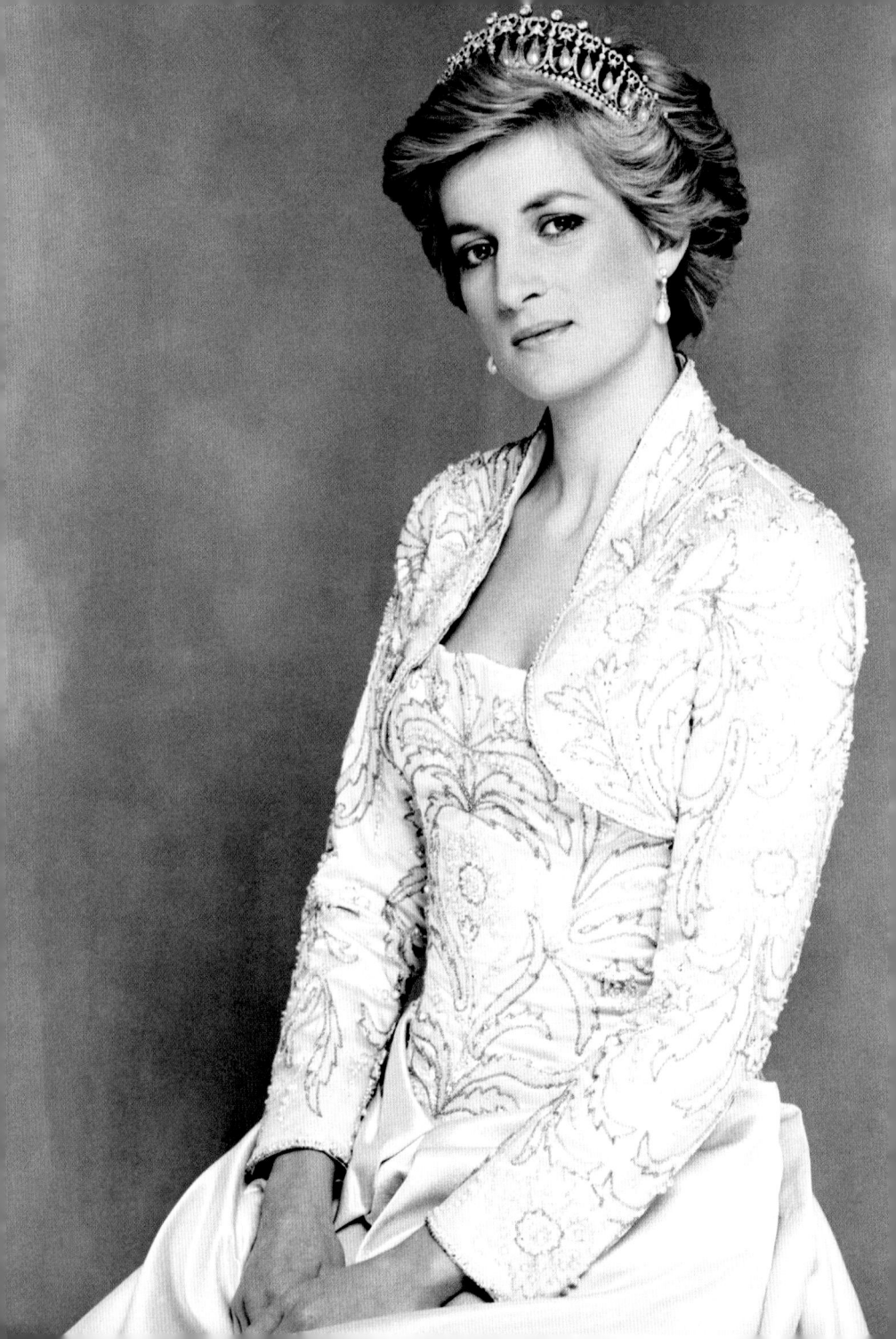

Diana, Princess of Wales
26 February 1990

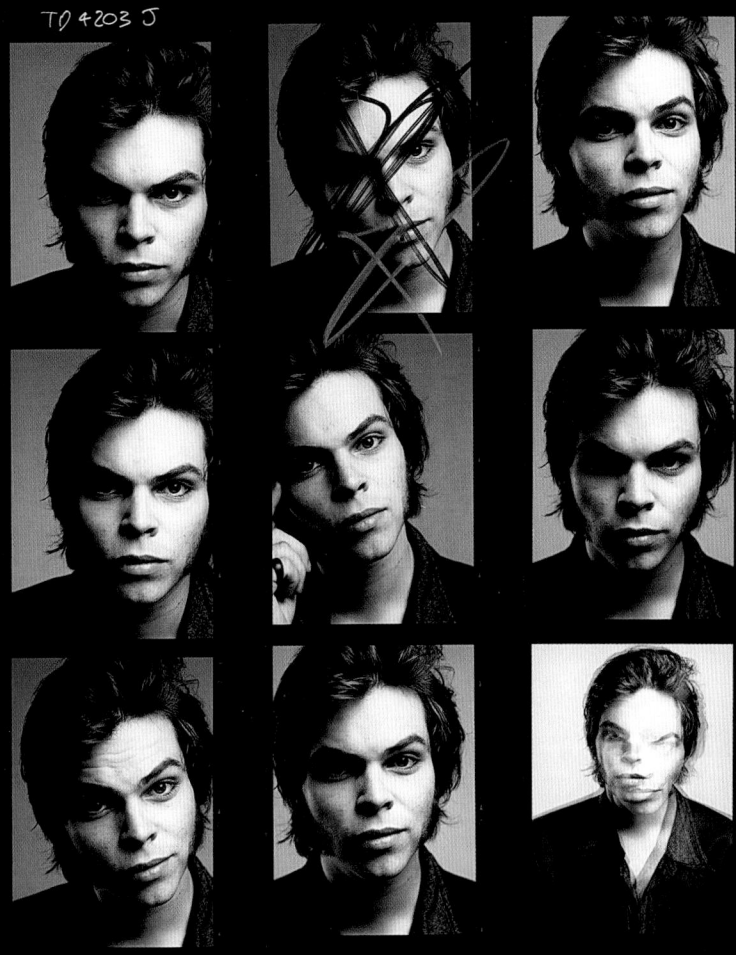

Gaz Coombes
GQ
December 1996

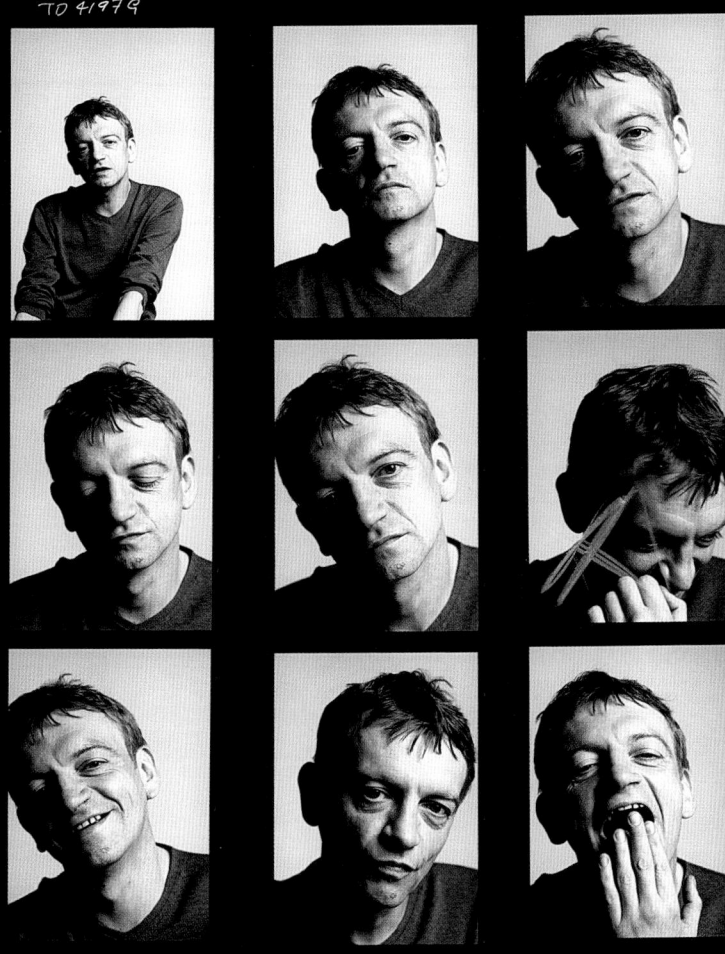

TO 41979

Mark E Smith
GQ
December 1996

Right
Frederick and
Arthur Gandolfi
c. 1985

Overleaf
House of God
The Que Club, Birmingham
20 January 1996

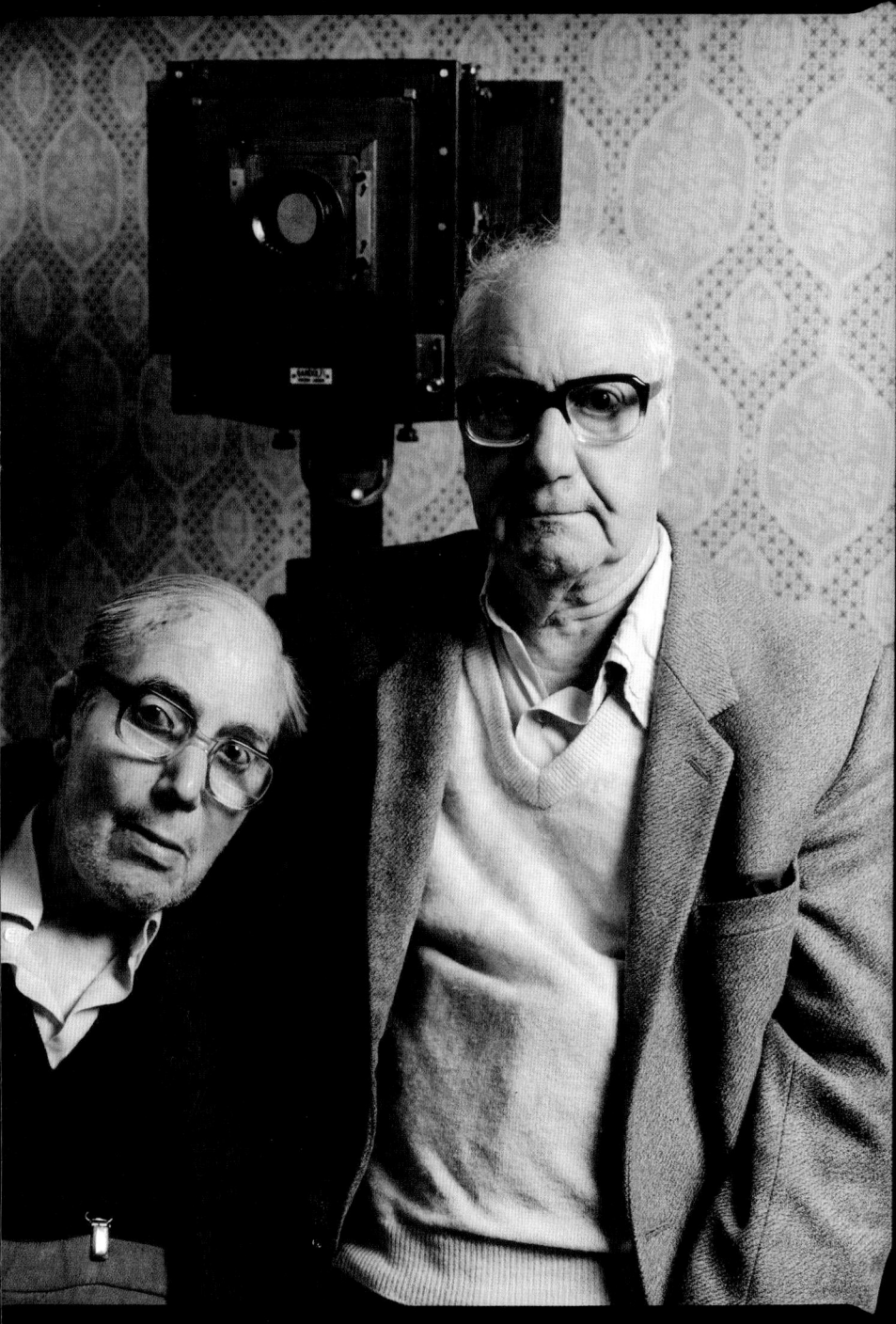

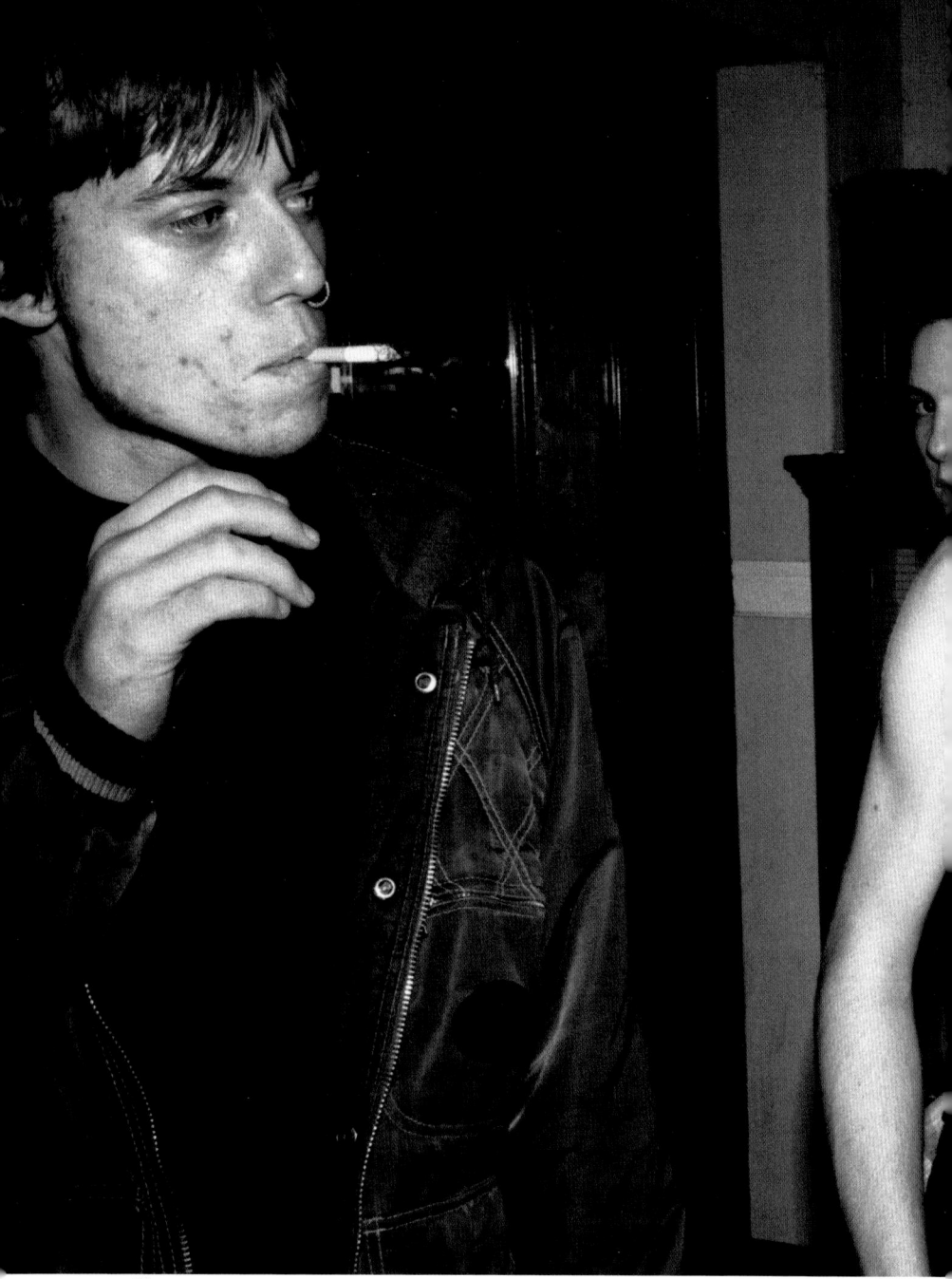

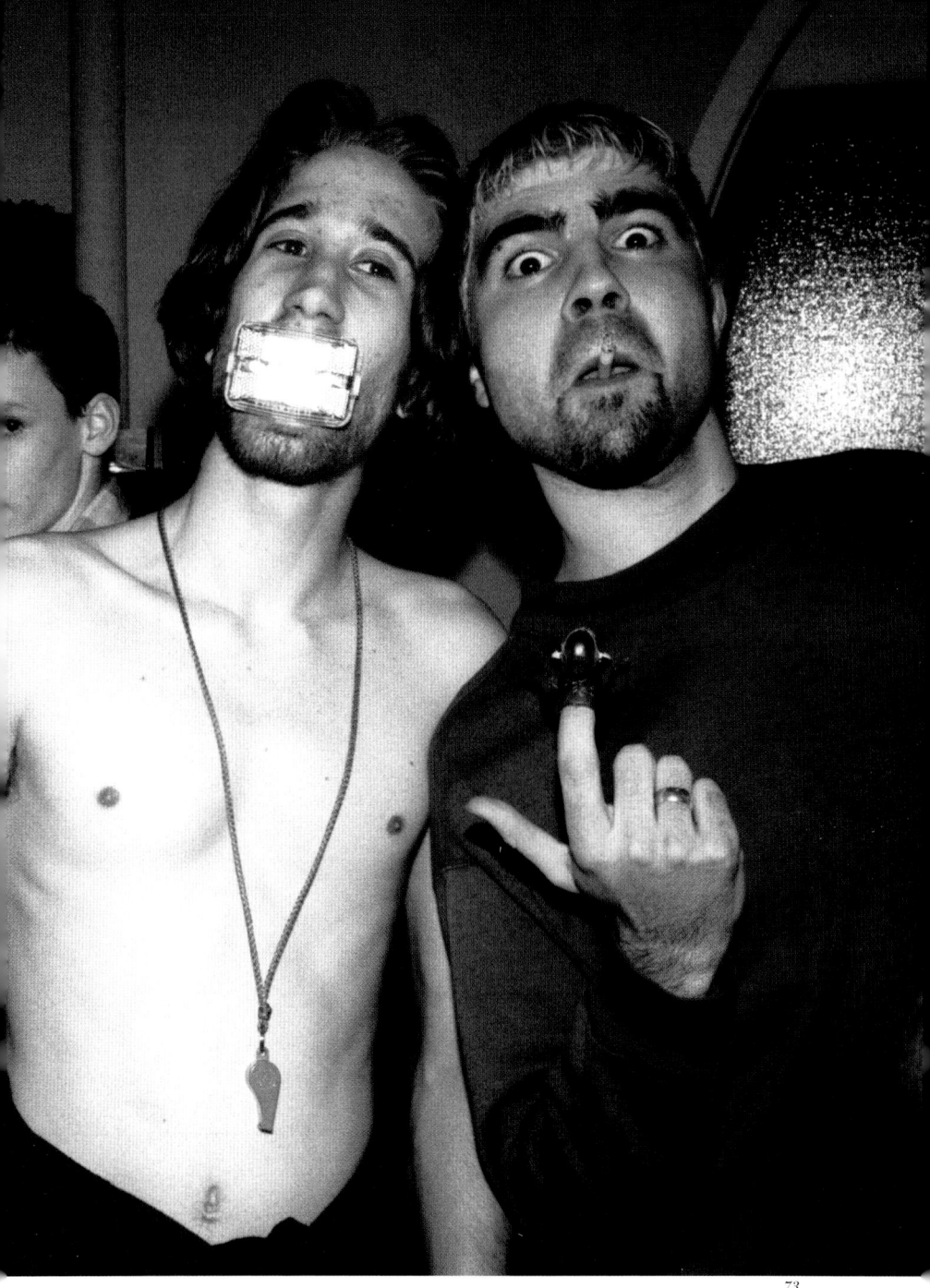

Marsha Hunt
23 December 1968

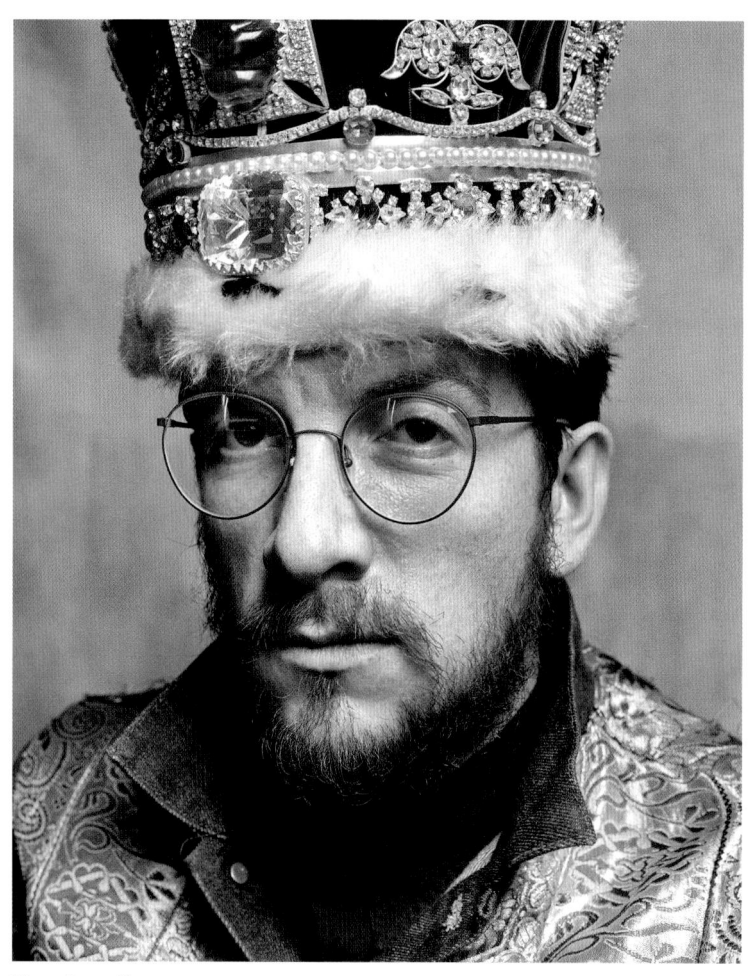

Elvis Costello
Album cover of *King of America*
8 August 1985

Liese Deniz
24 November 1959

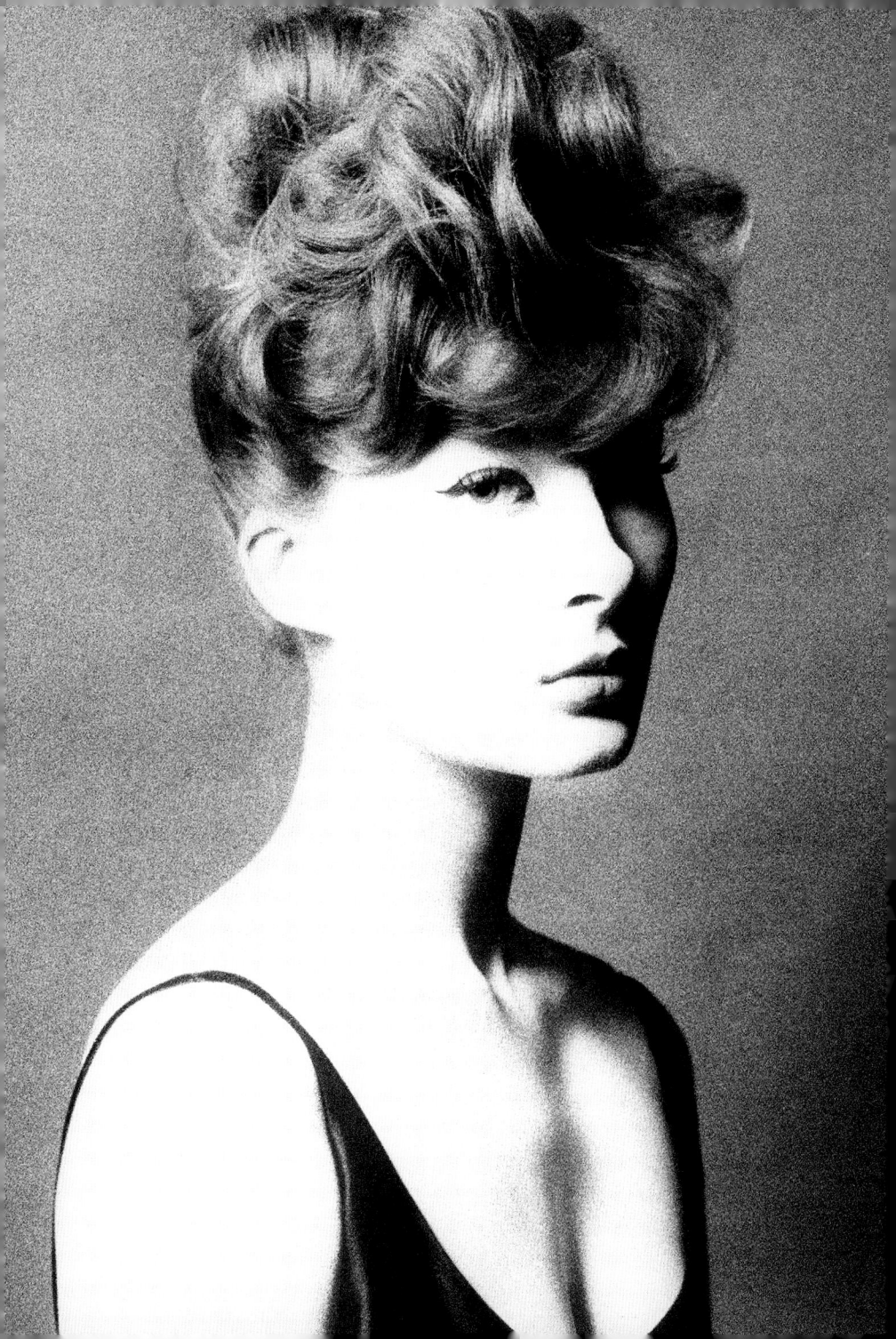

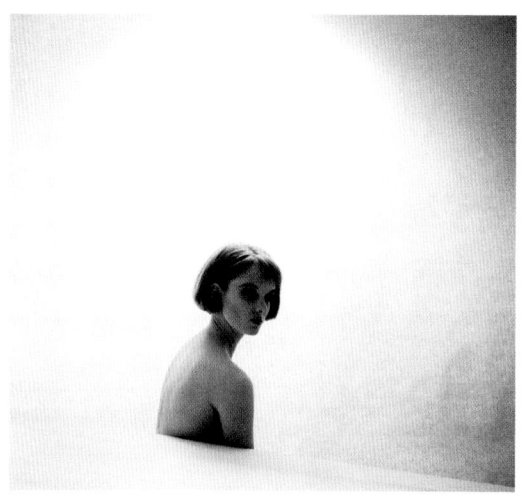

Grace Coddington
7 December 1960

Right
Sylvie Guillem
4 June 1993

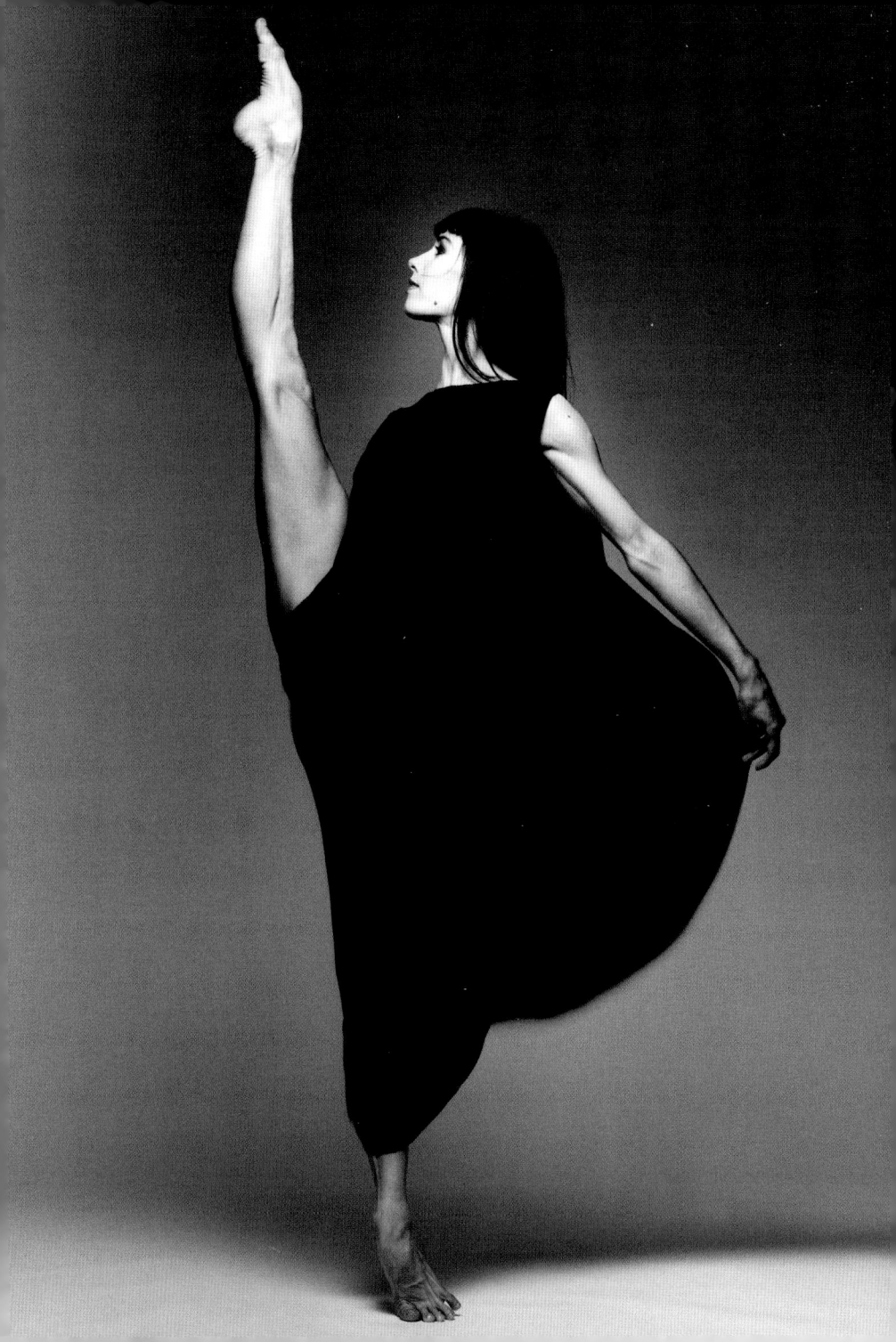

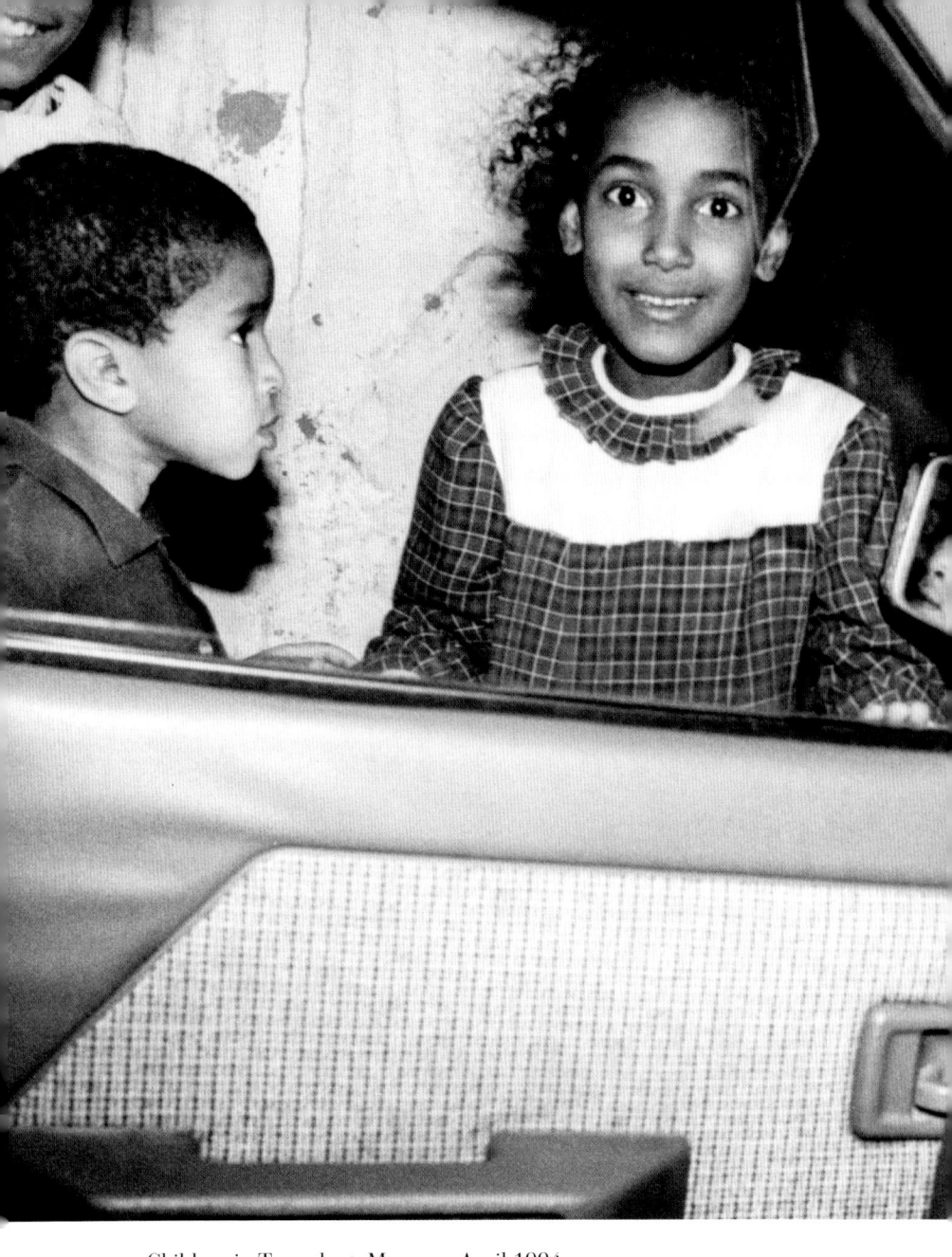

Children in Taroudant, Morocco, April 1994

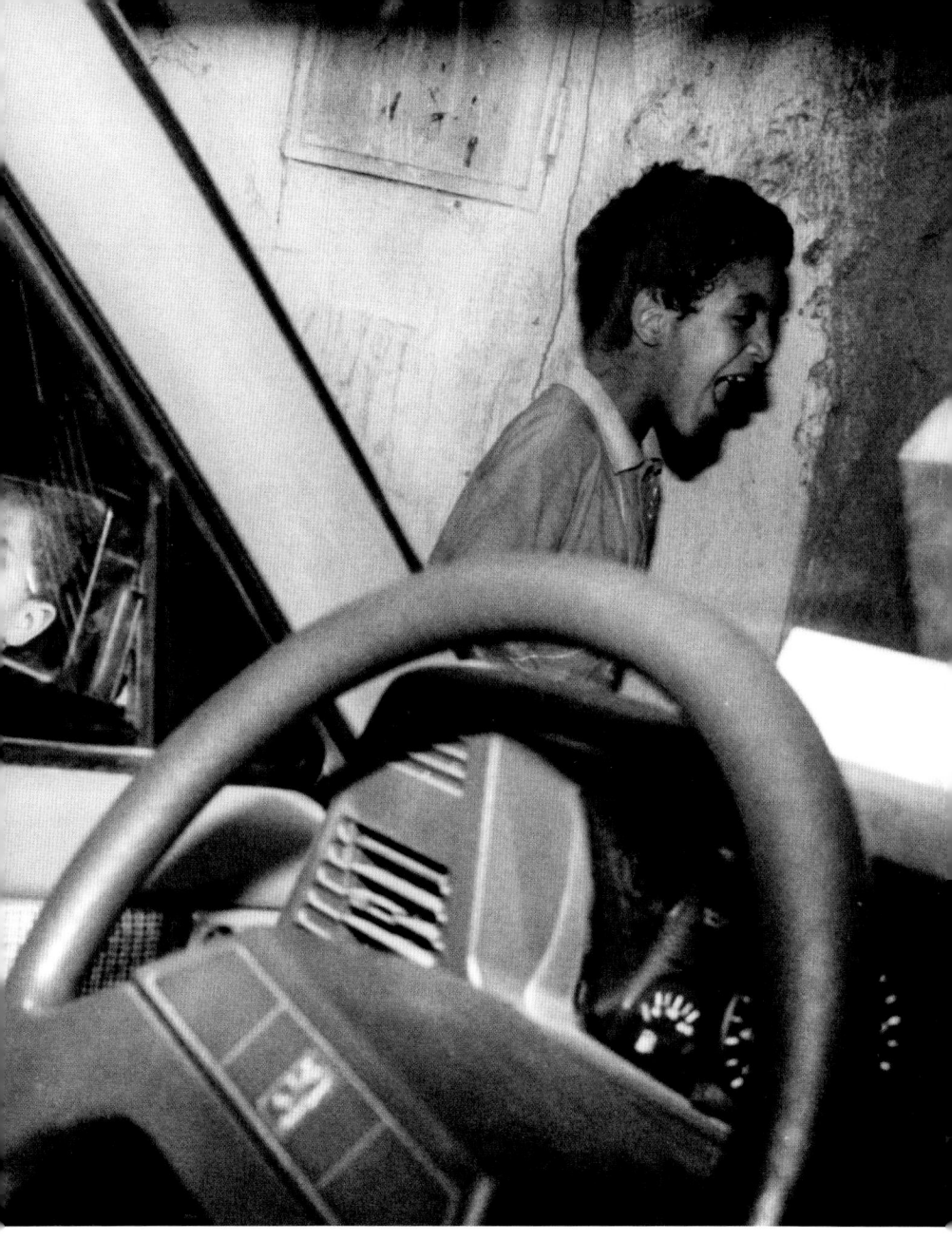

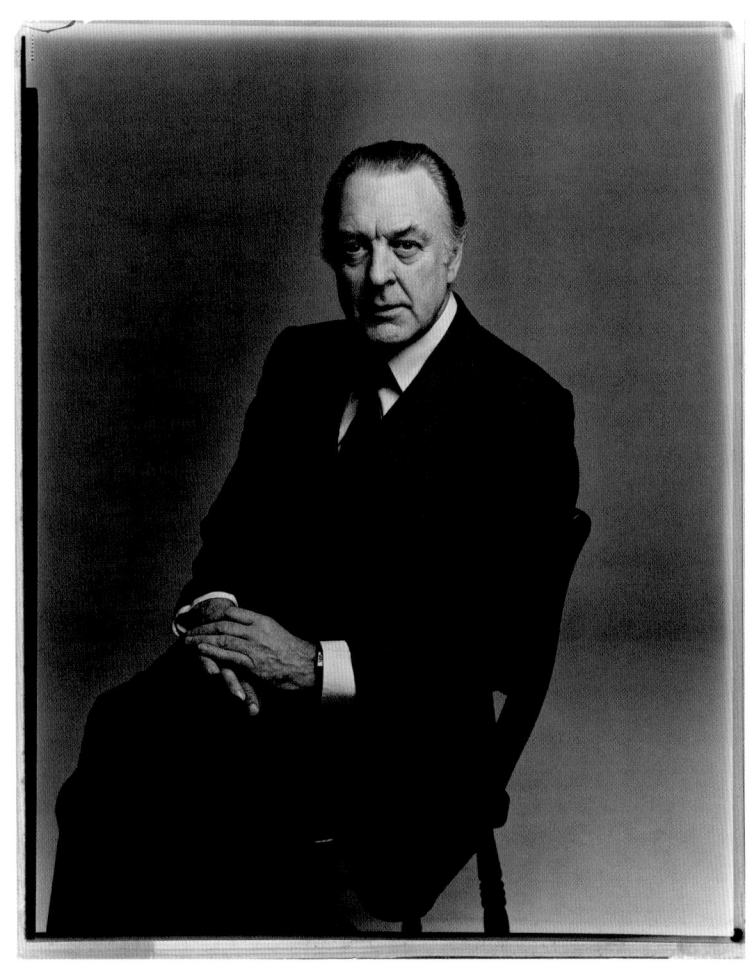

Donald Sinden
Over 21
14 December 1981

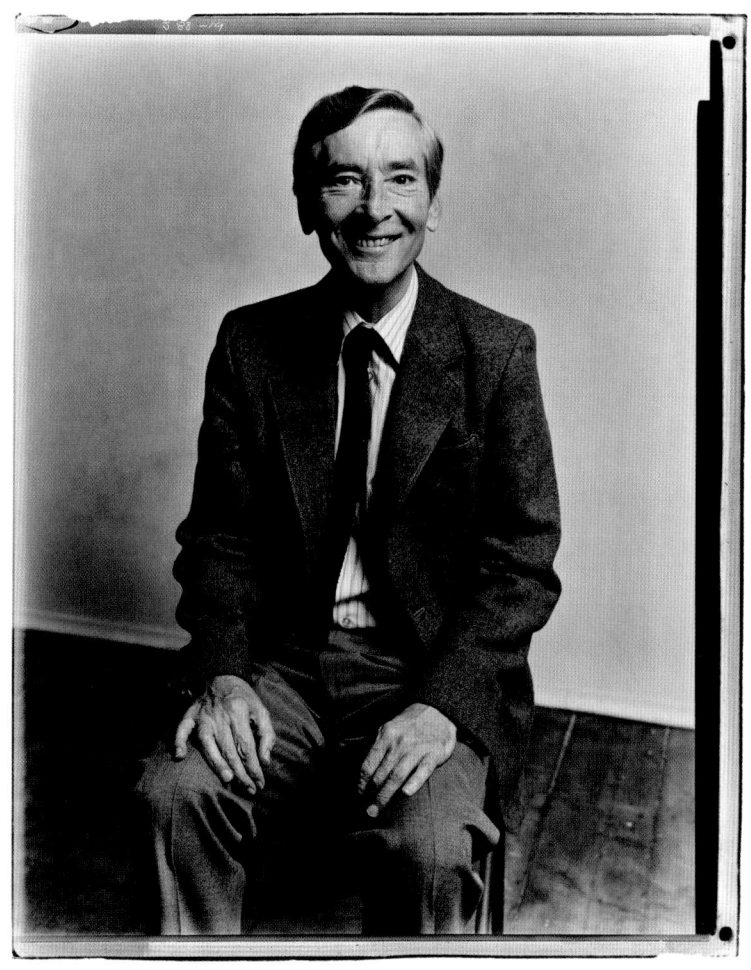

Kenneth Williams
28 September 1981

Overleaf
Susan Davis
24 August 1966

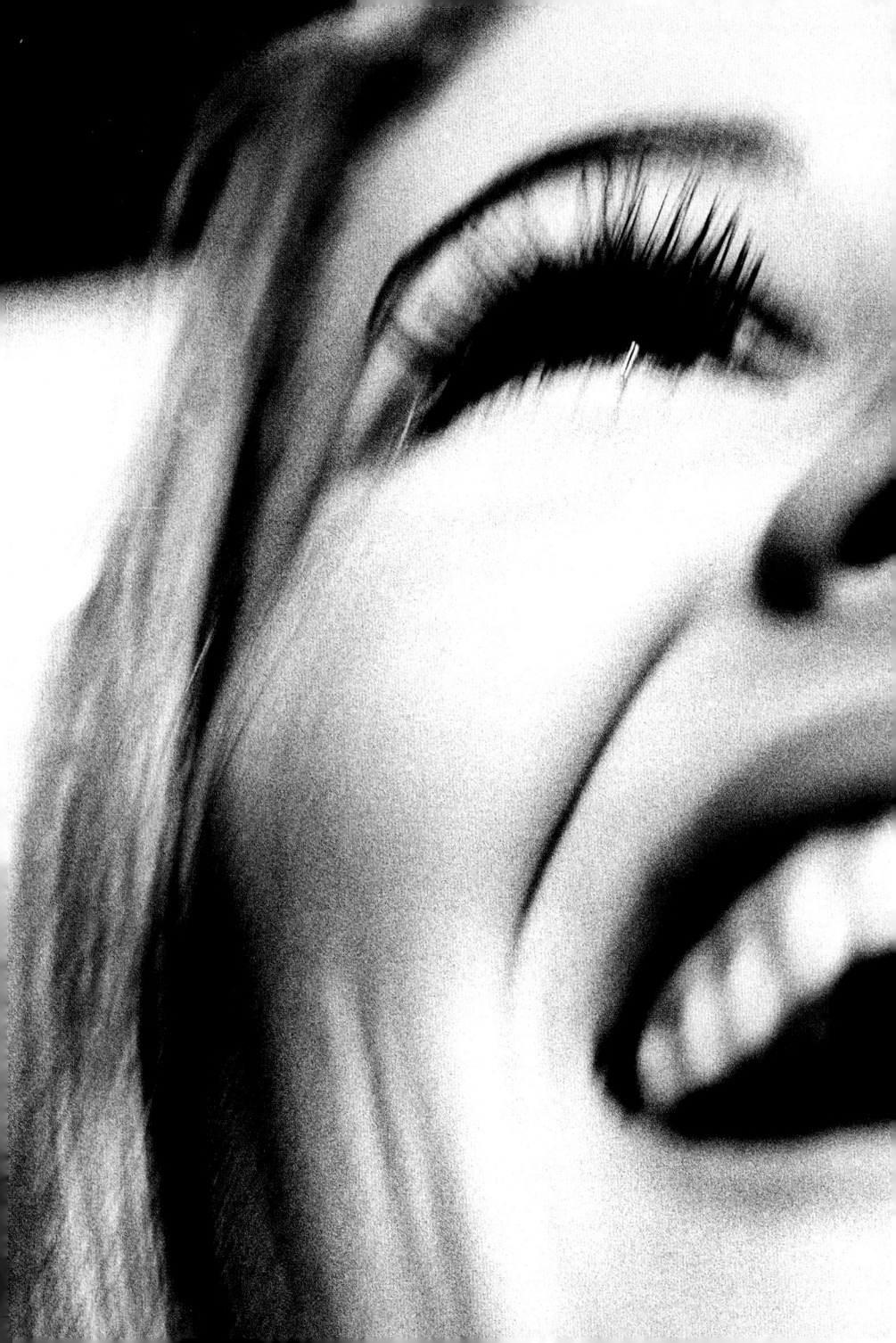

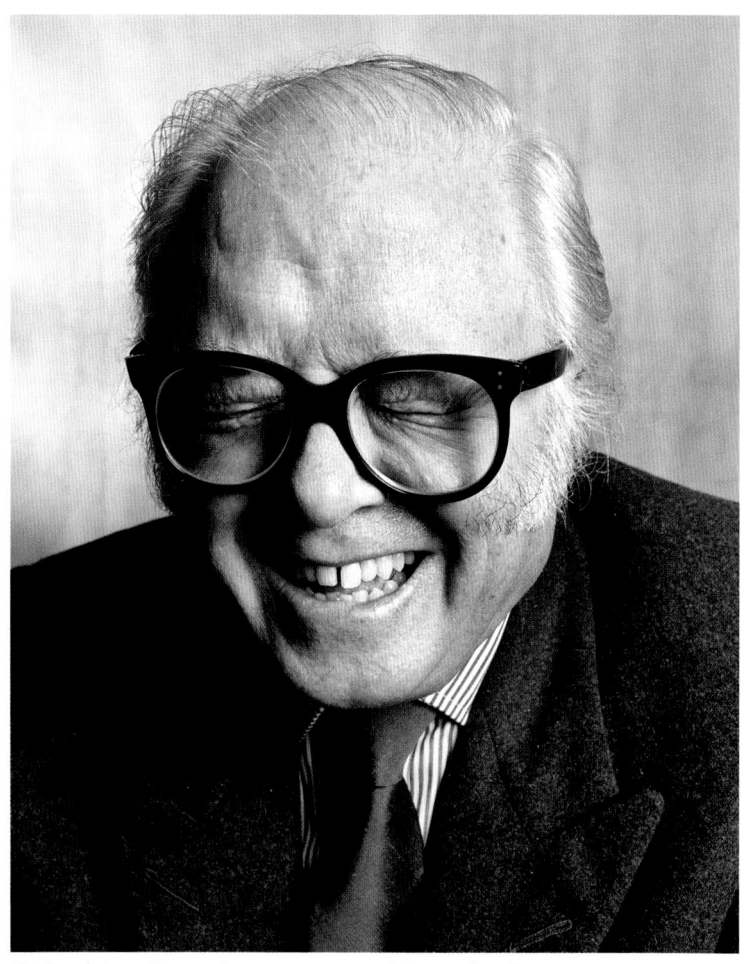

Richard Attenborough
Sunday Express Magazine
21 October 1987

Maggie Smith
Harper's Bazaar
10 April 1964

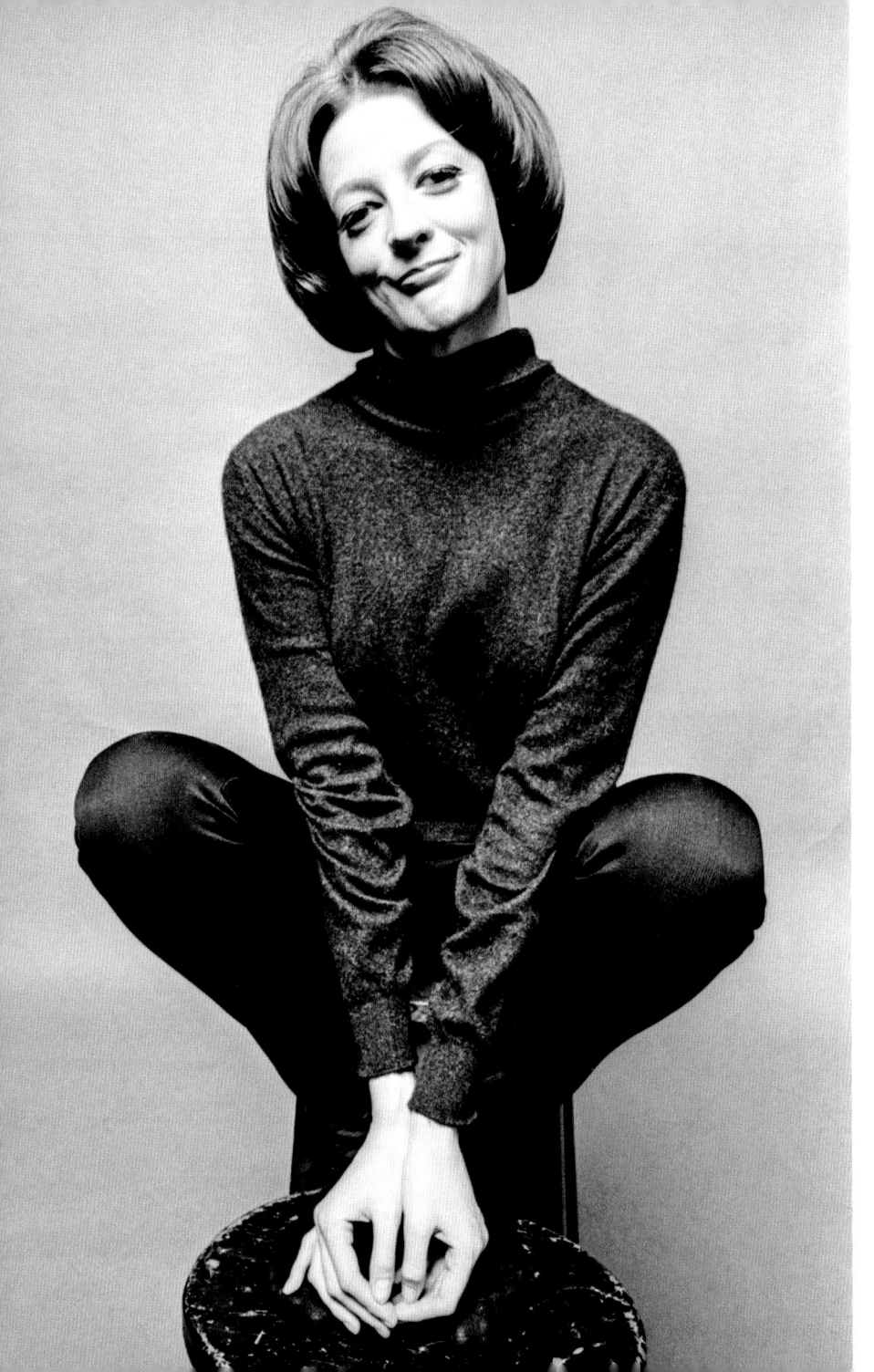

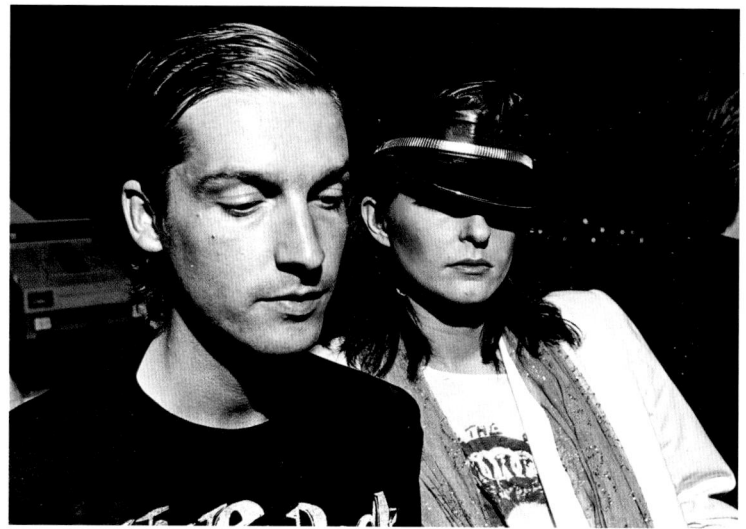

Jack English and Helen Robinson
The Embassy Club
c.1978

Below, The Myers Twins
London Life
20 July 1965

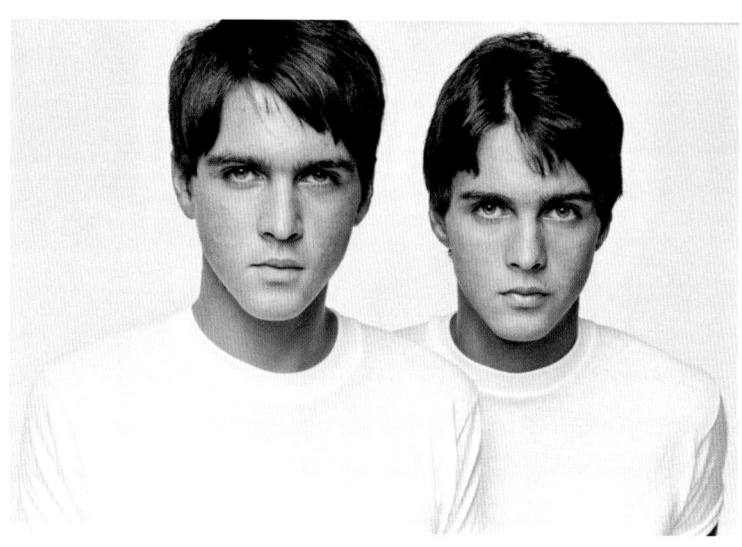

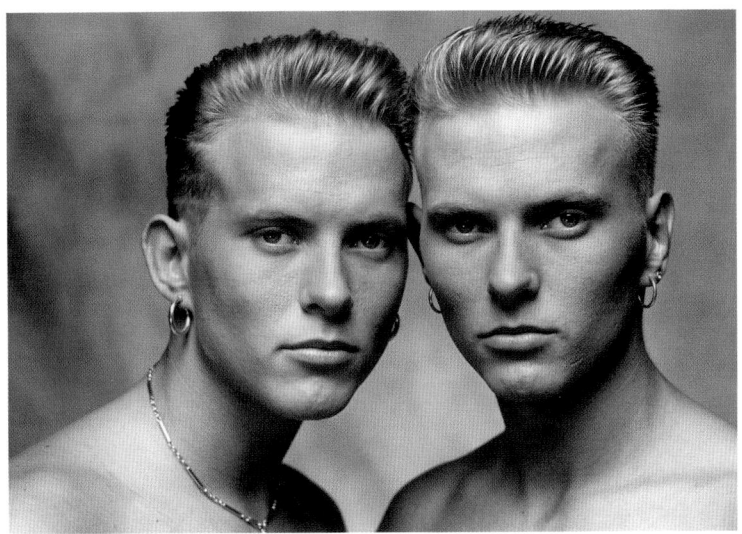

Bros (Matt and Luke Goss)
19 July 1989

Below, Pet Shop Boys
7 September 1990

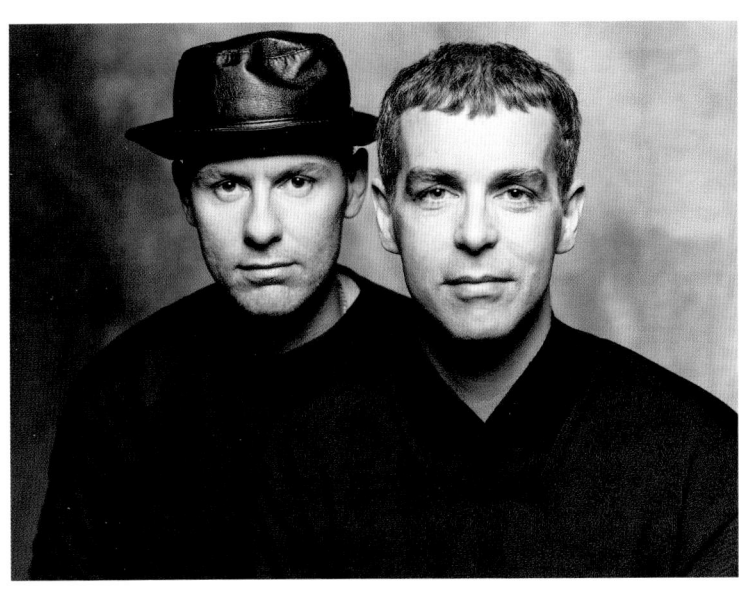

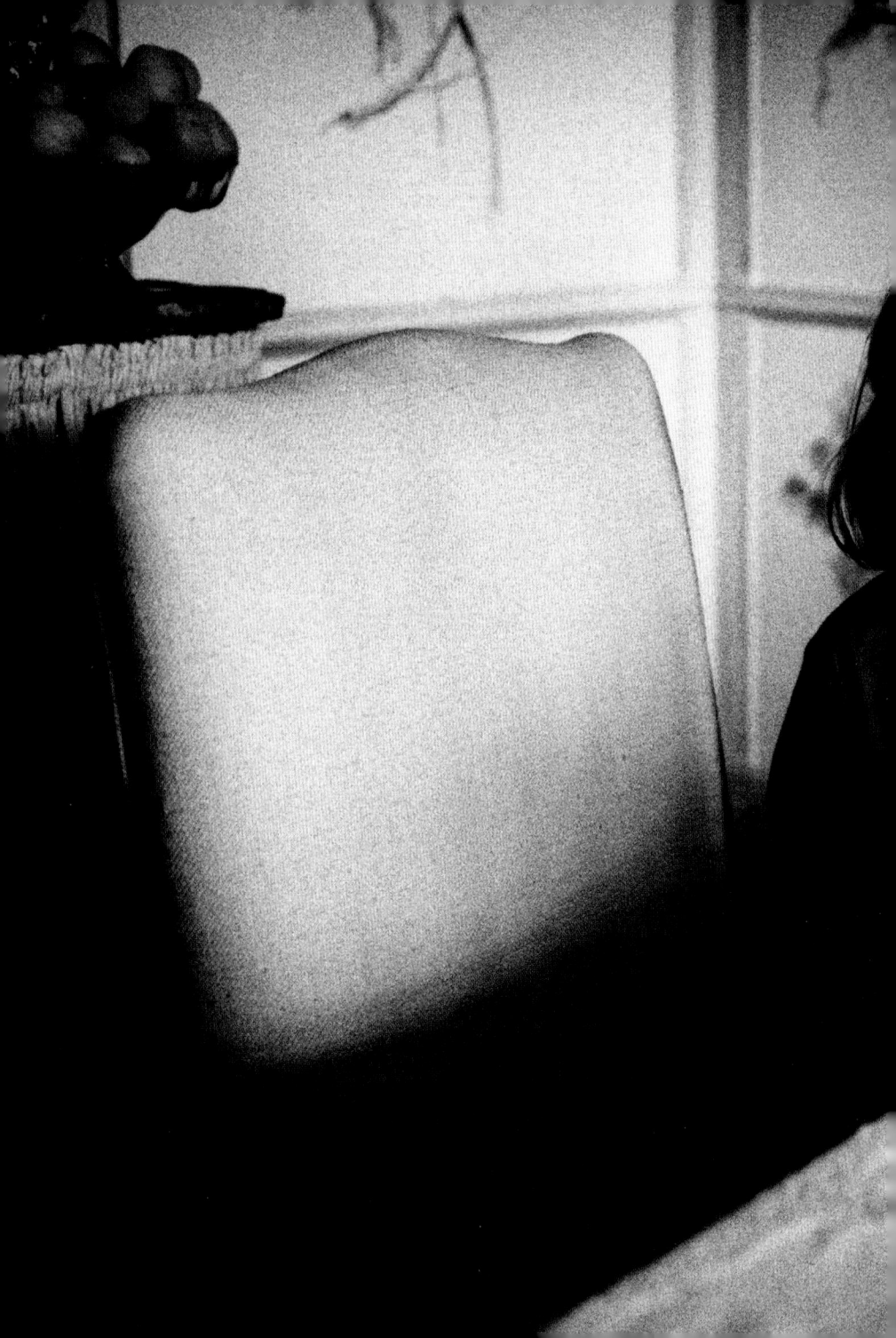

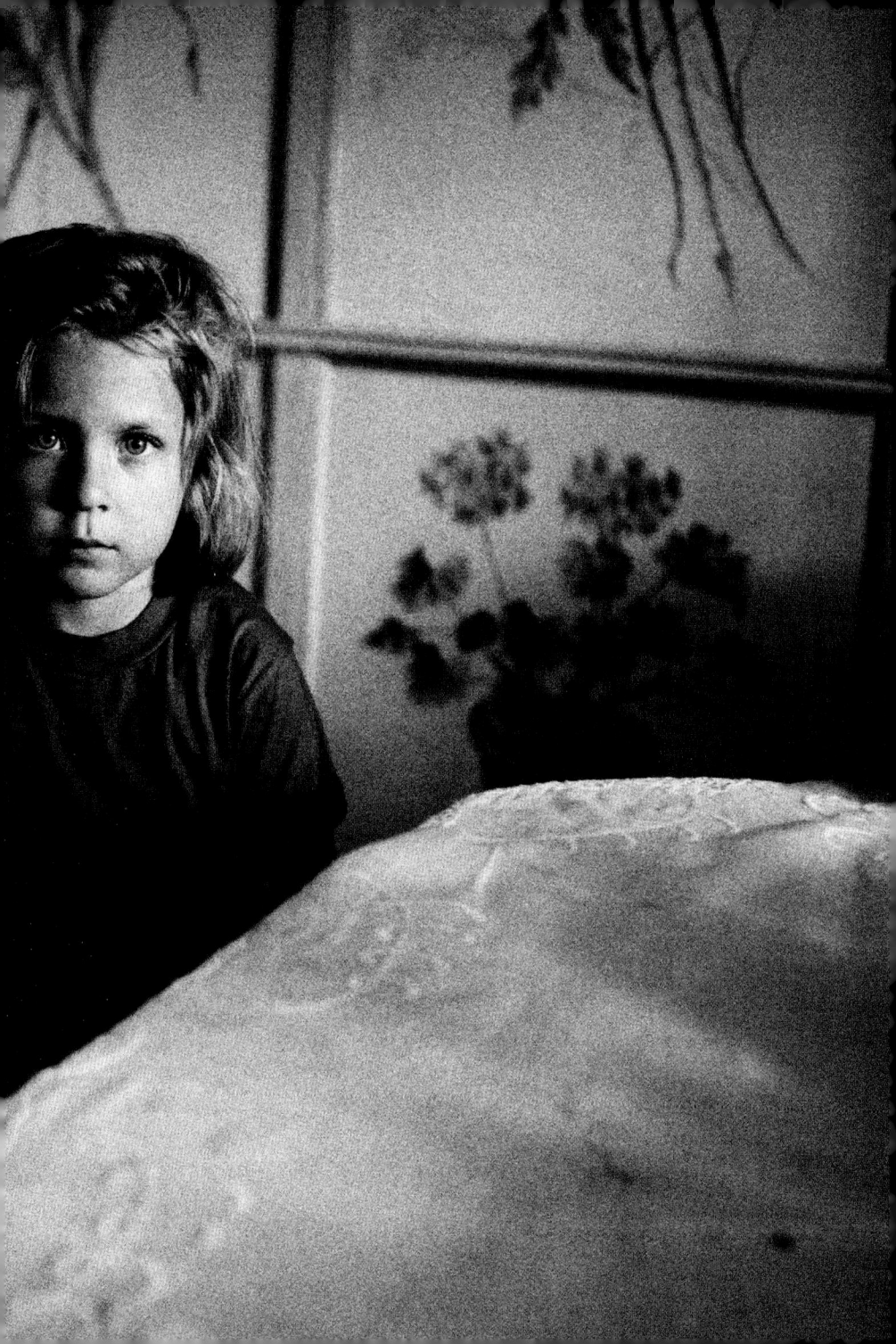

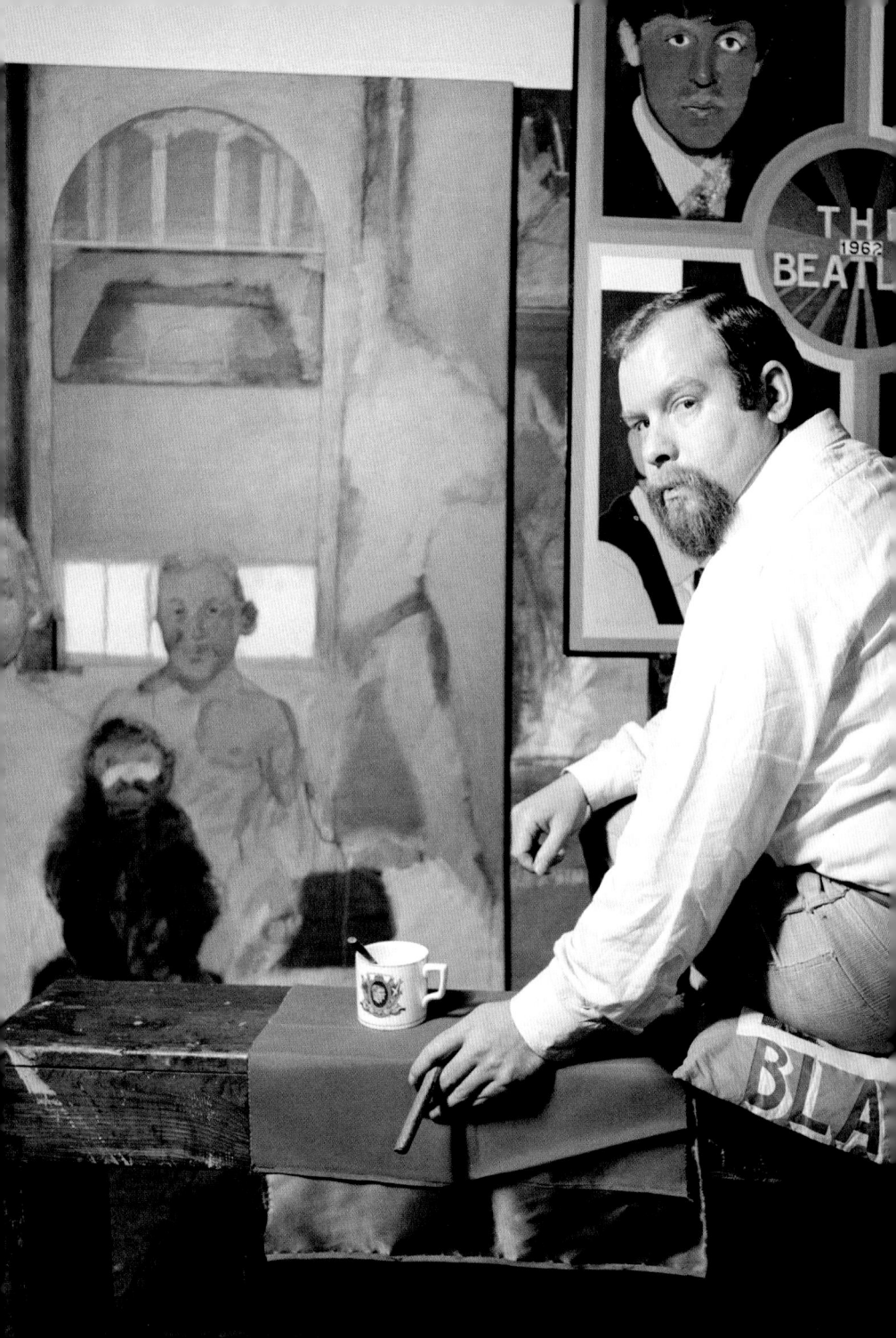

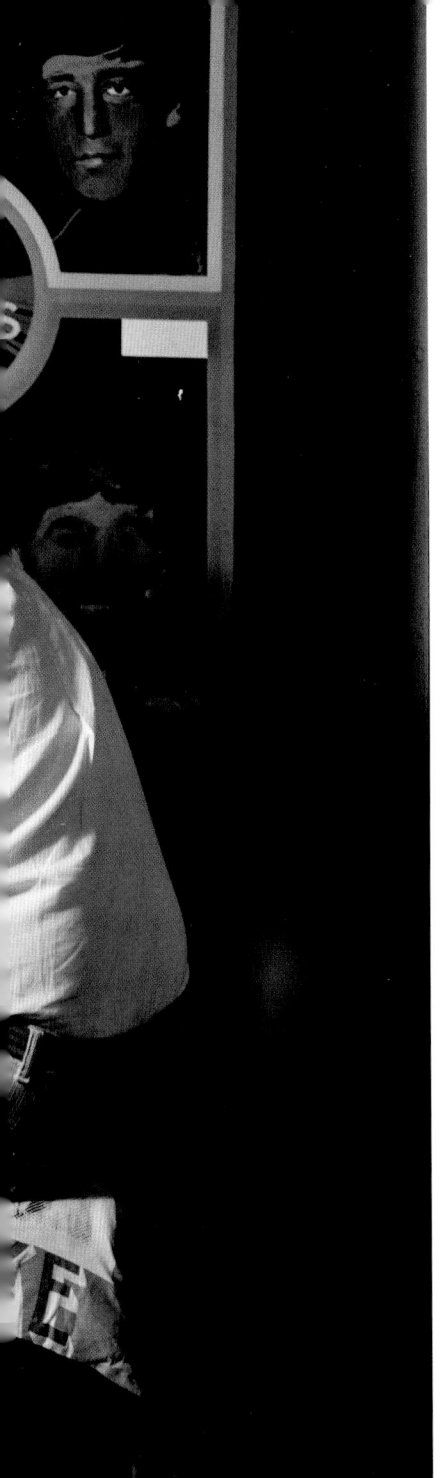

Preceding page
Skye McAlpine
June 1989

Left
Peter Blake
September 1965

Overleaf
Bernardo Bertolucci
17 July 1989

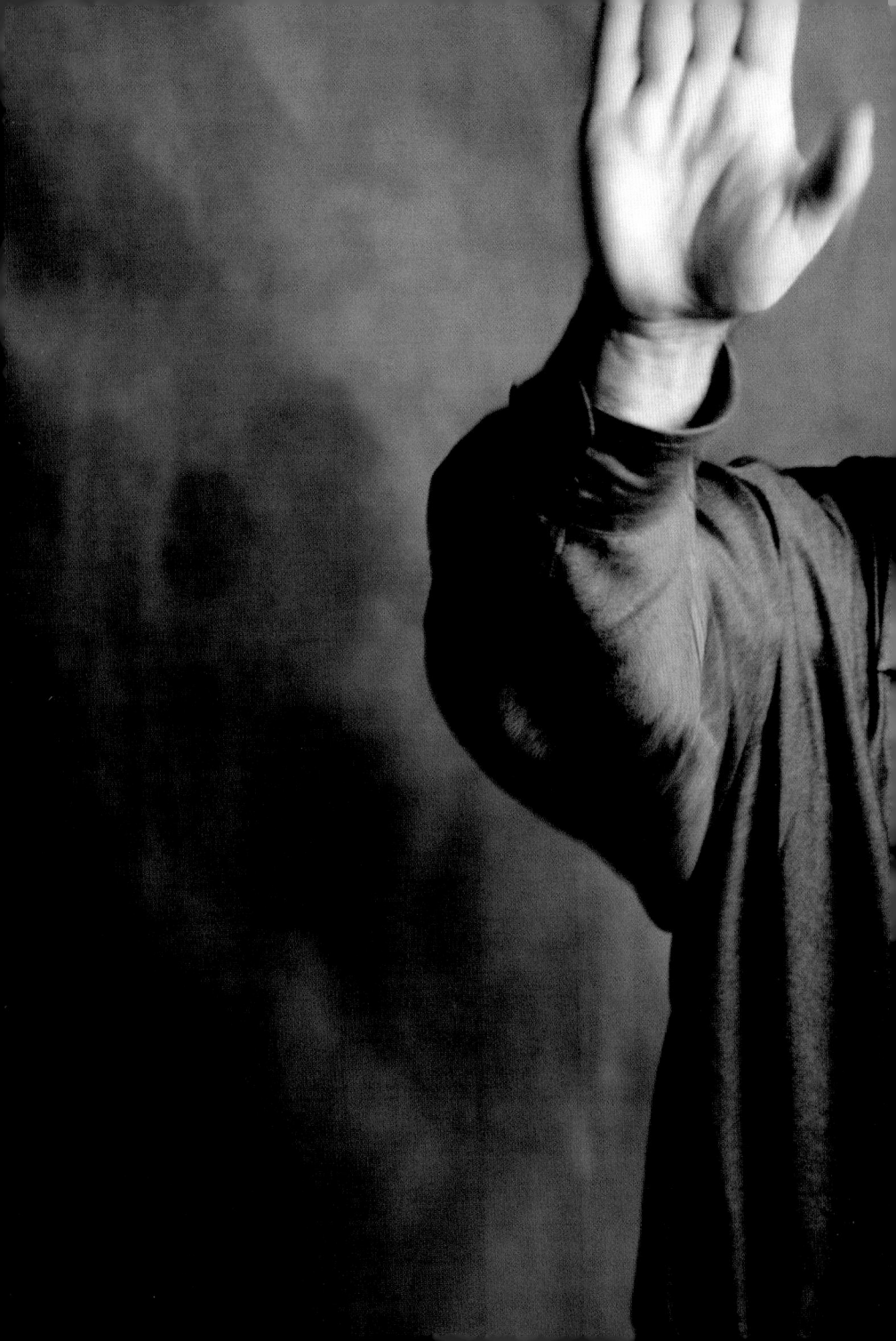

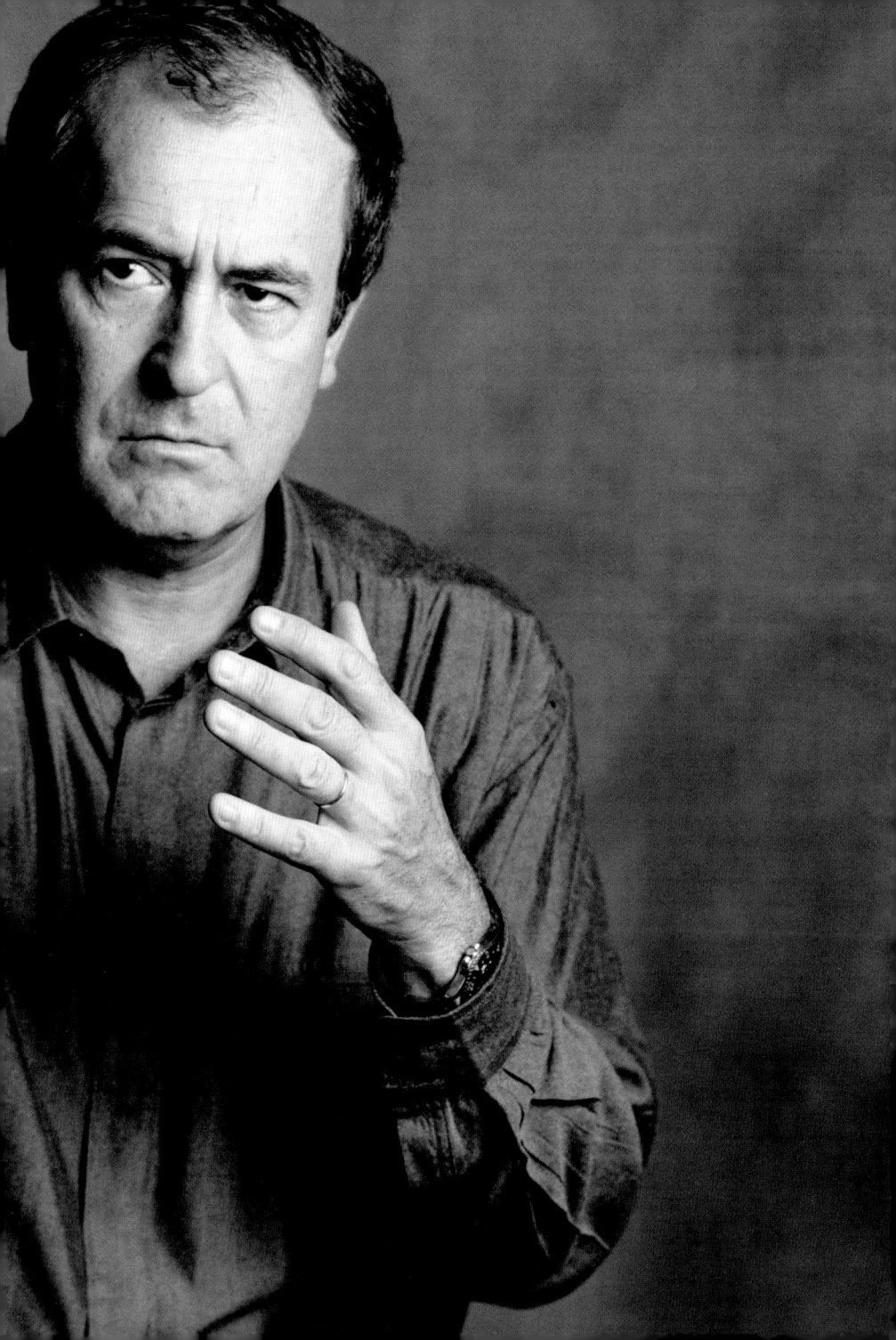

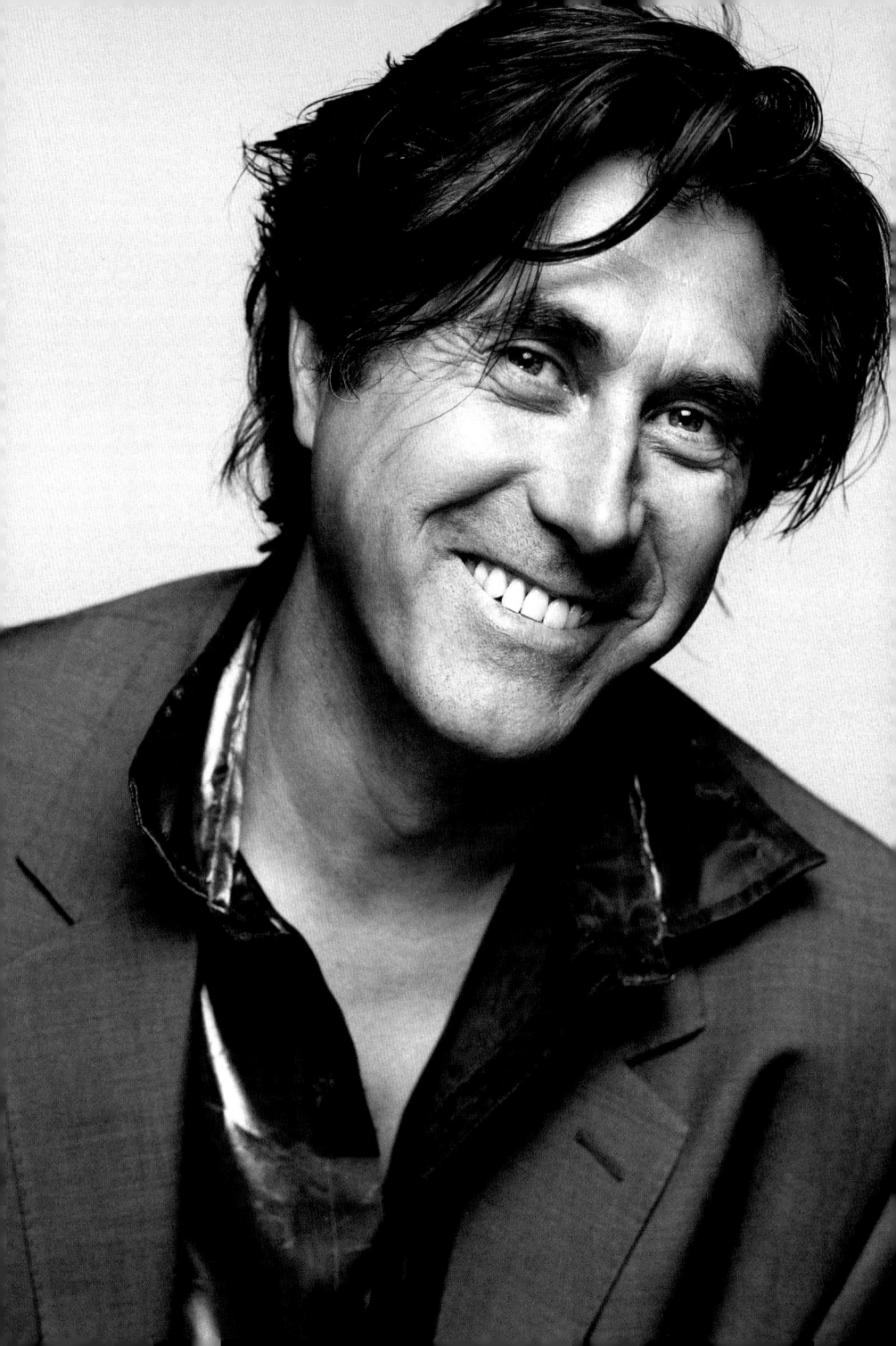

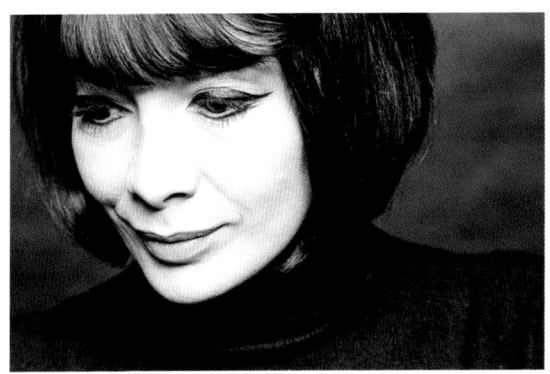

Juliette Gréco
London Life
8 November 1965

Left
Bryan Ferry
GQ
December 1996

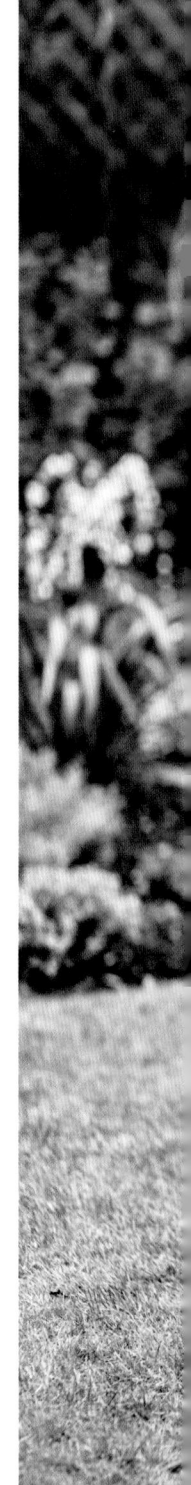

Dan, Daisy and Terry Donovan
c.1978

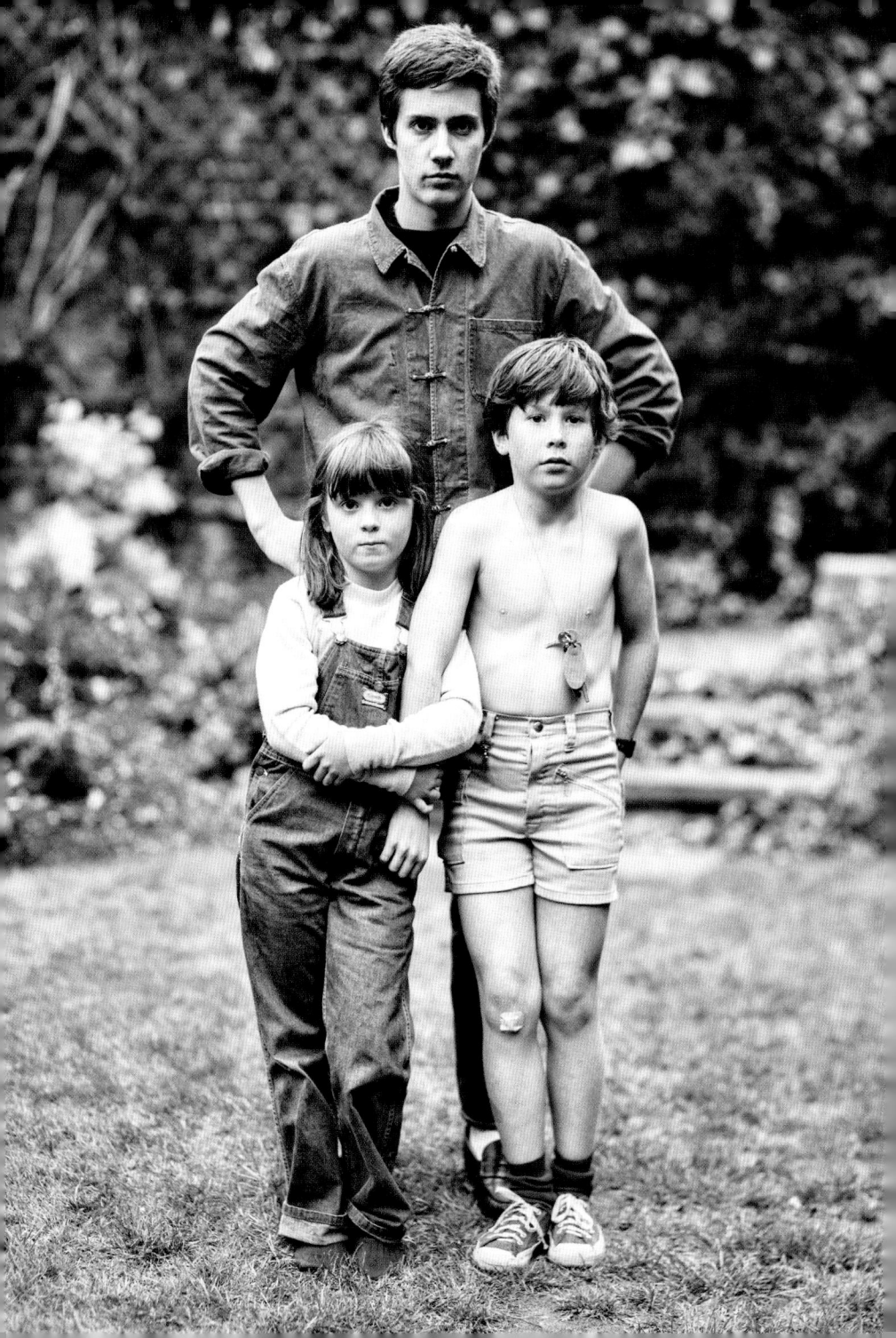

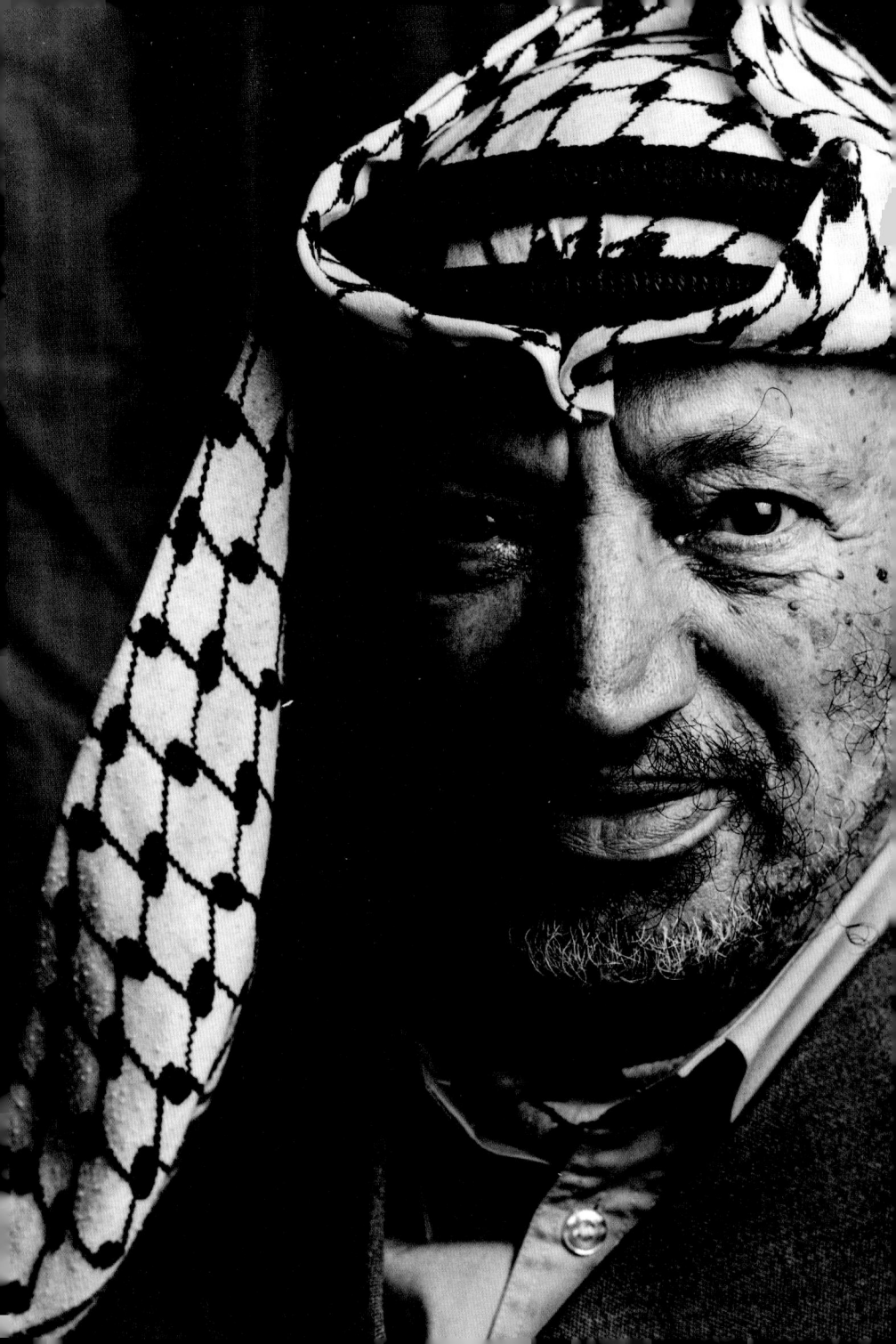

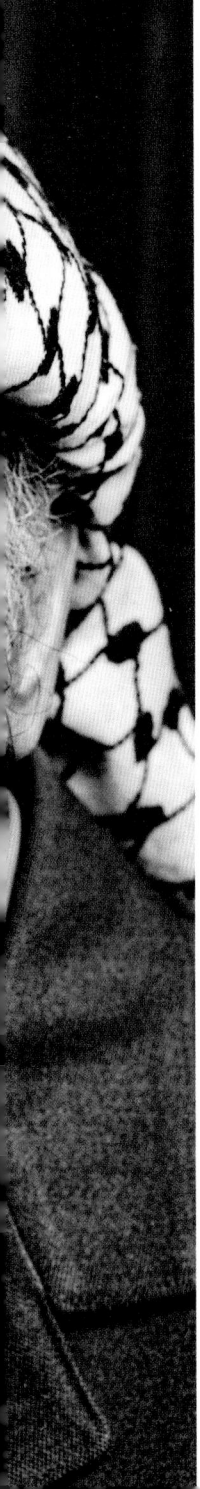

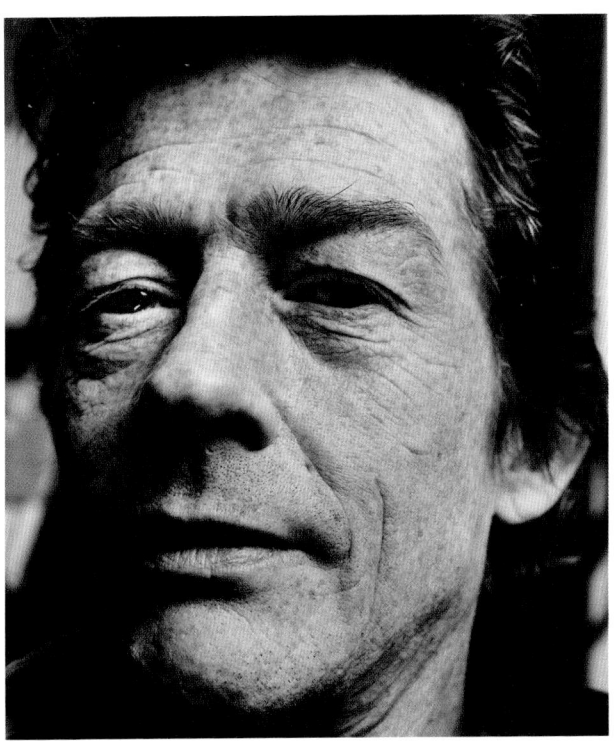

Yasser Arafat
June 1996

Above
John Hurt
Punch
14 May 1985

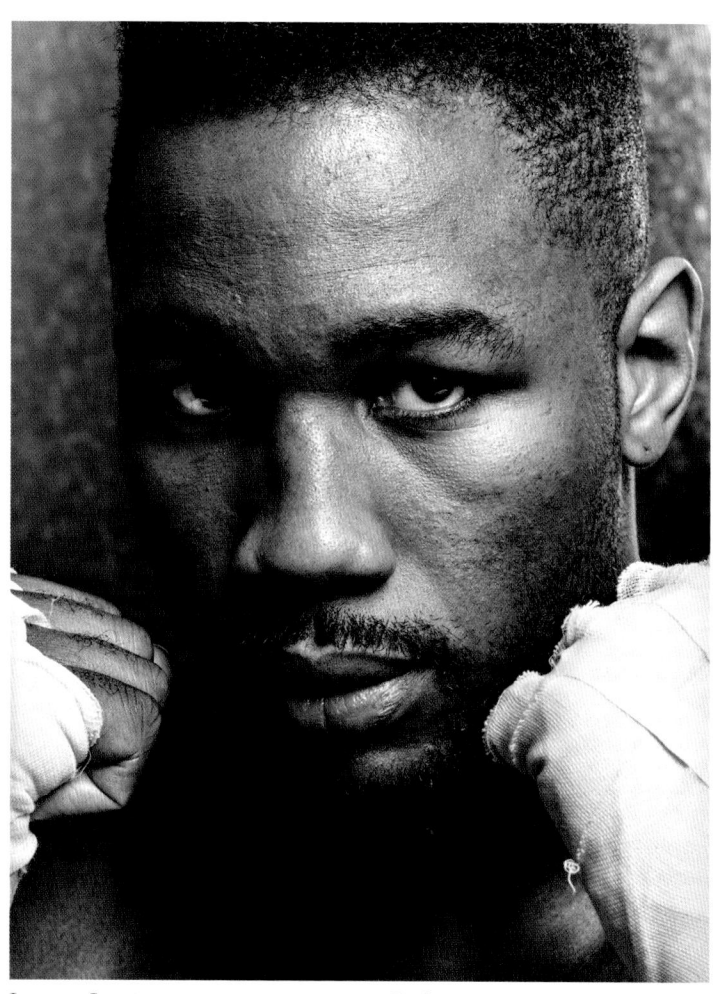

Lennox Lewis
US *Harper's Bazaar*
3 December 1992

Right
Henry Cooper
Ritz
31 January 1978

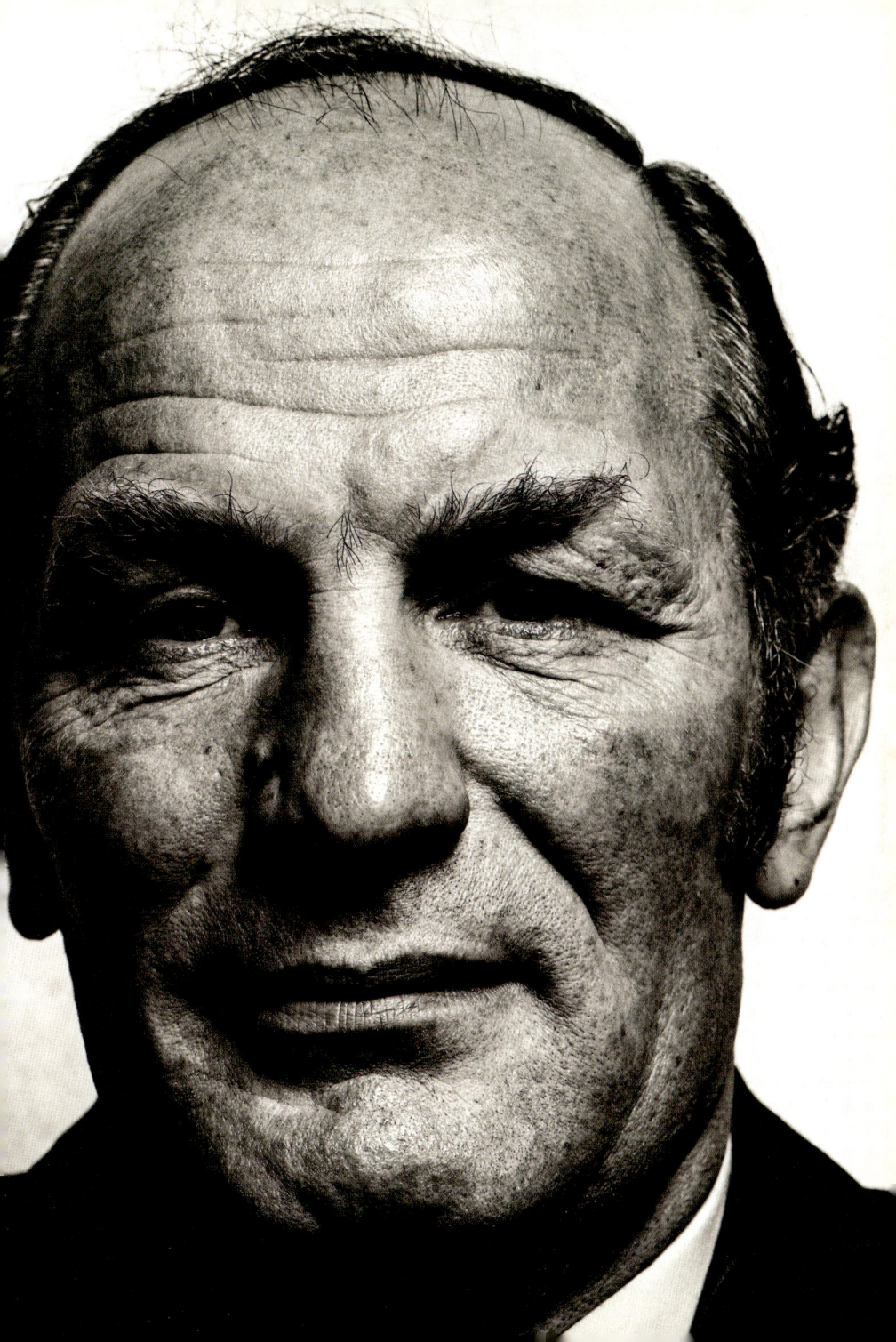

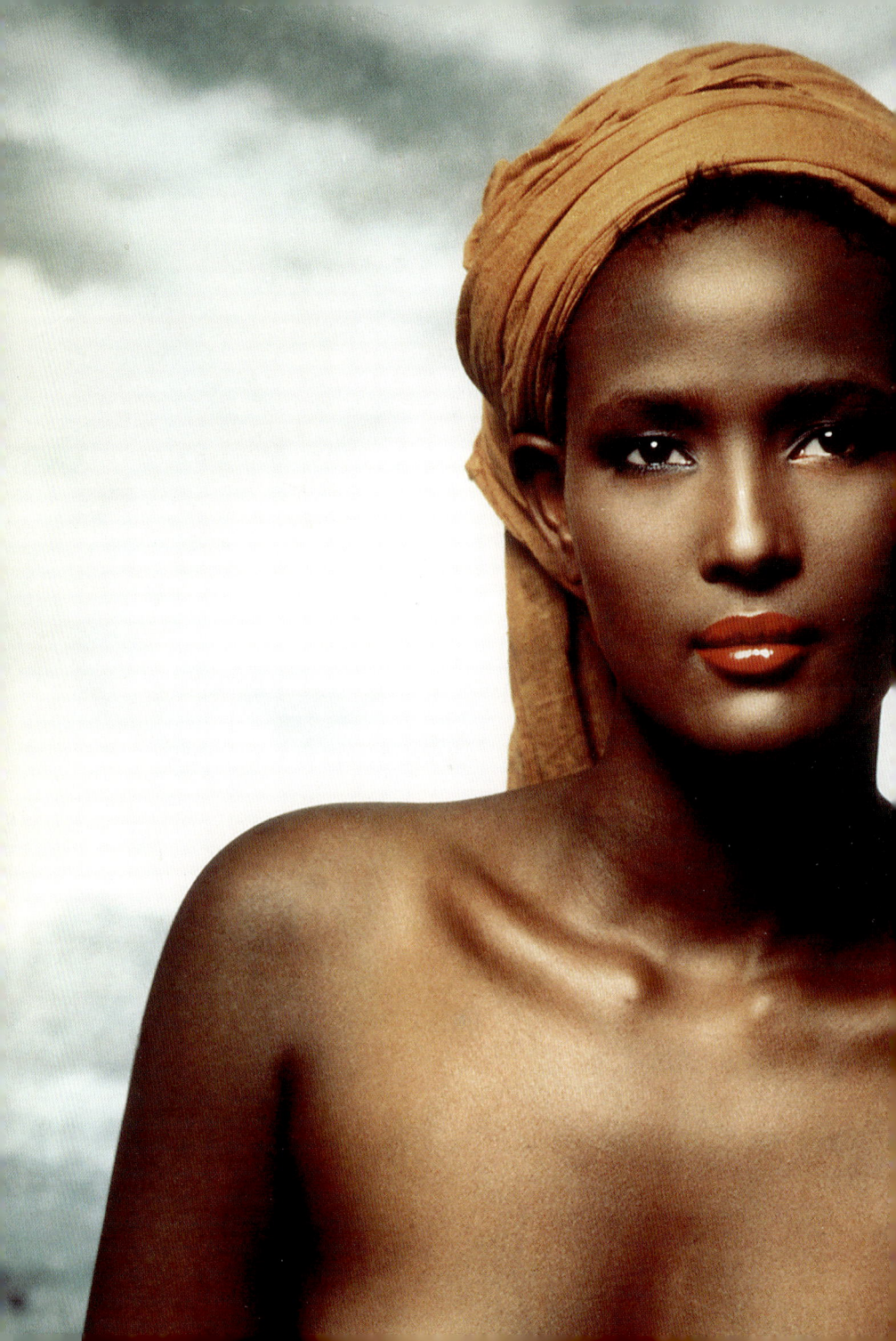

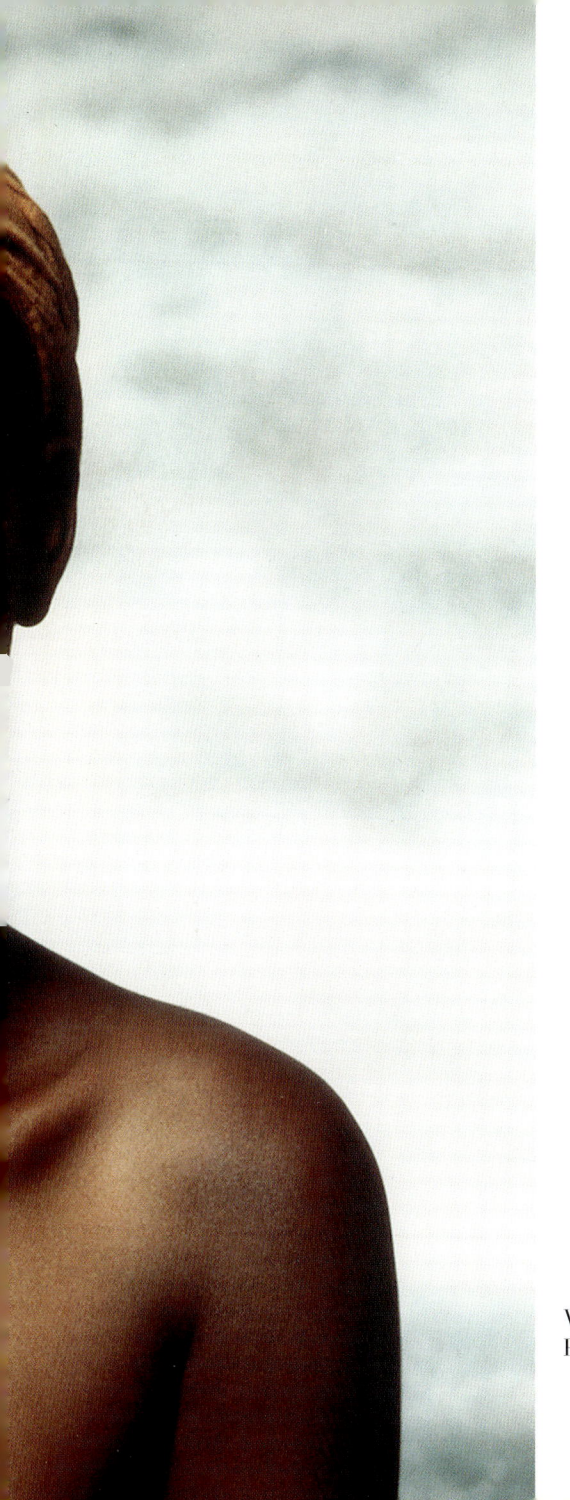

Waris Dirie
Pirelli Calendar 1987

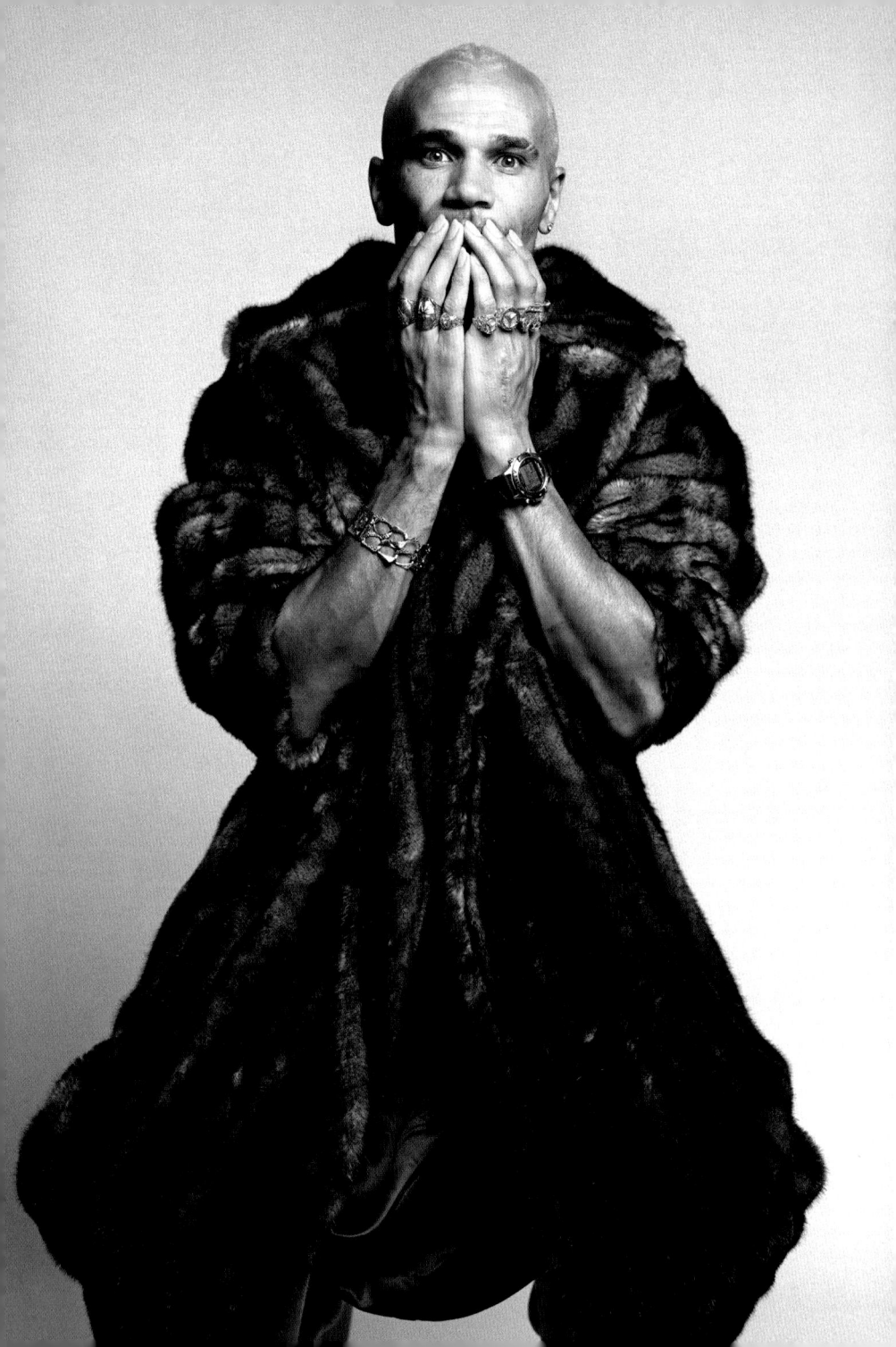

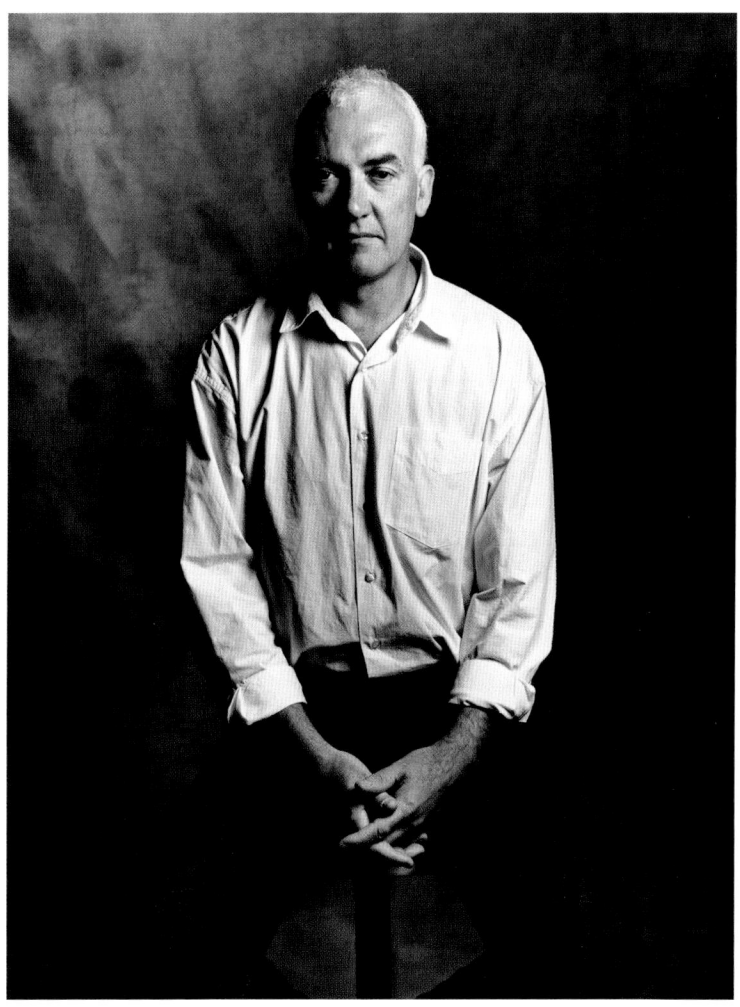

Goldie
GQ
December 1996

Above
Sean Scully
19 September 1992

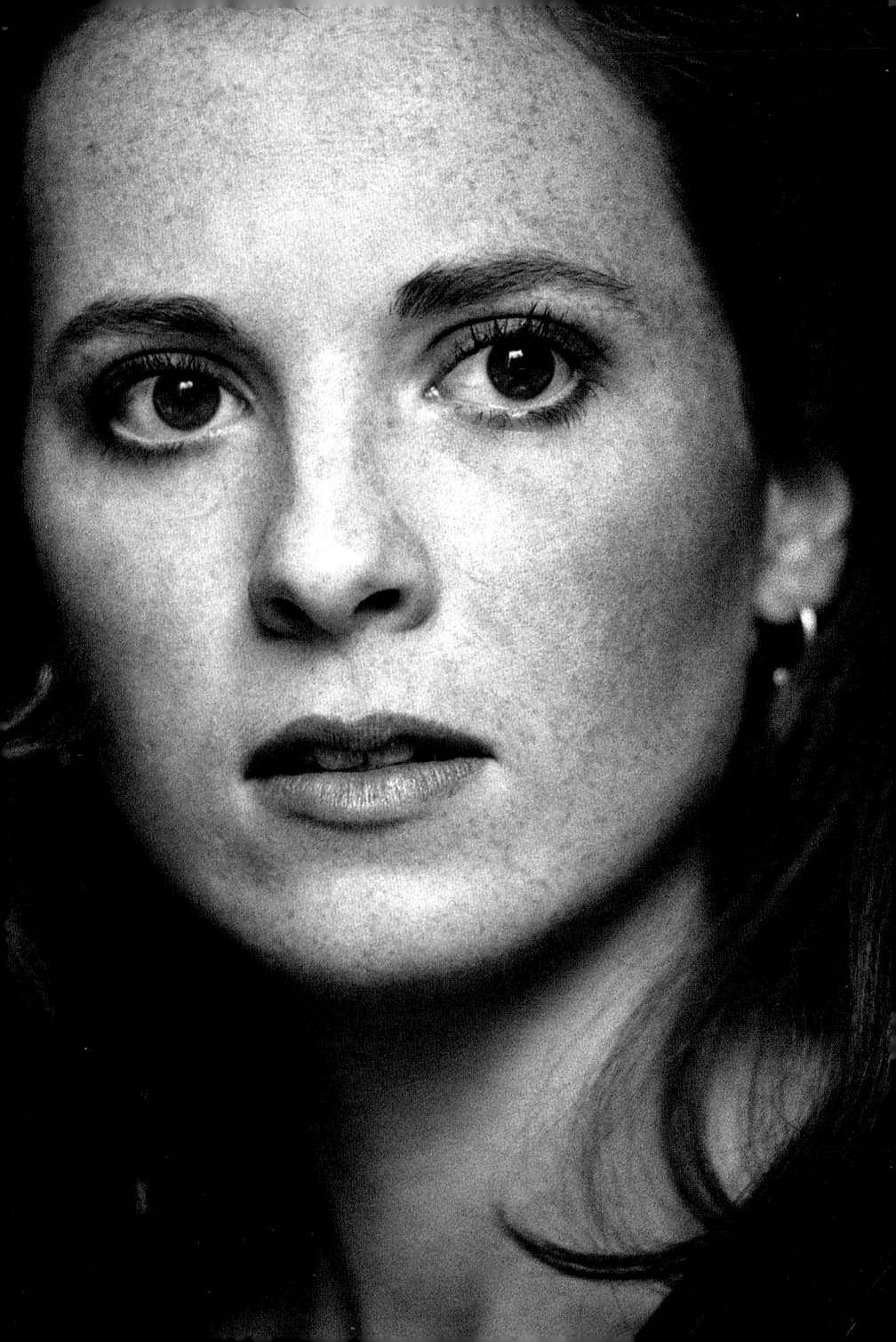